For our grandchildren
Sebastian, Amelia, Harry and Isabelle
in the hope that they will see, in their lifetime,
a world free from children's institutions.

ॐ

And in memory of
Anna Dawson and Harry Henderson
who were greatly loved,
and Catarina who was not.

Hope & Homes for Children
East Clyffe, Salisbury
Wiltshire, SP3 4LZ
United Kingdom

ISBN 978-0-9930655-0-7
First Published 2014 by Mark & Caroline Cook

Typeset in 11 on 16pt Palatino

Editor: Audrey Paisey
Book design & layout by Simon Howden - allthings creative

Printed in Great Britain by Colourview, Salisbury
Cover printed on 350gsm Regency Satin White FSC ®
Text printed on 150gsm Regency Satin White FSC ®
Printed using vegetable based inks

*The photograph on the cover of this book was taken inside an institution in Moldova
by Alexandra Smart. Alexandra spent the first two and a half years of her life in an
institution in Romania until she was rescued by a loving family.
She graduated in Documentary Photography from the University of Wales, Newport.
Alexandra has also been a volunteer for Hope and Homes for Children
working in the East Clyffe office.*

Hope & Homes for Children

ACKNOWLEDGEMENTS

We would like to thank the following people without whose great help and encouragement we would have found it extremely difficult, if not impossible, to write this book.

Audrey Paisey has been a totally committed volunteer in our East Clyffe office for 15 years and has visited our programmes in five countries. Her knowledge of Hope and Homes for Children has been invaluable, as well as her professional experience in higher education and the training of teachers. Audrey has given an enormous amount of her time in the last six months helping in the development of the book and by meticulously editing every draft – and there have been many!

Helen Tyson, our ultra-efficient Assistant for the last five years, has been amazingly patient in typing numerous drafts without any hint of exasperation!

James Ruddy came out on many visits to various countries with us when he was the Deputy Editor of the *Eastern Daily Press* newspaper. He has been a great help to us with content, design, and layout.

Our designer, Simon Howden of allthings creative, could not have been more helpful and supportive.

Mark & Caroline.

We are guilty of many errors, and many faults
But our worst is abandoning the children;
Neglecting the fountain of life.
Many of the things we need can wait.
A child cannot.
Right now is the time his bones are being formed,
His blood is being made,
His senses are being developed.
To him, we cannot answer, "Tomorrow"
His name is TODAY

Gabriela Mistral, the Chilean Nobel Prize-winning poet

Mrs Woolley,

With our great thanks for your wonderful support over the last 15 years, and our very best wishes

Mark & Caroline.

A Silent Cry
for love

Saving children from darkness and despair

By Mark & Caroline Cook

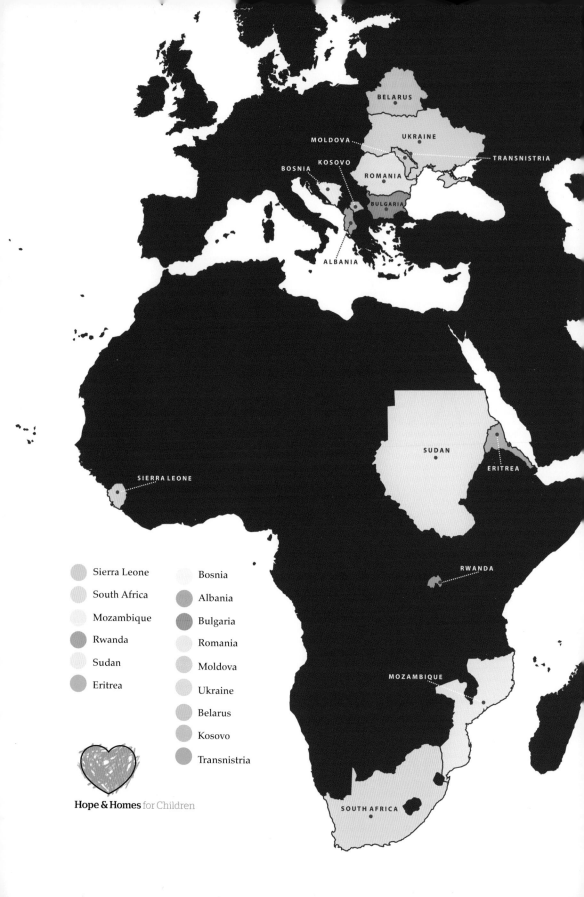

BELARUS

MOLDOVA   UKRAINE

TRANSNISTRIA

KOSOVO

BOSNIA   ROMANIA

BULGARIA

ALBANIA

SUDAN

ERITREA

SIERRA LEONE

RWANDA

MOZAMBIQUE

- Sierra Leone
- South Africa
- Mozambique
- Rwanda
- Sudan
- Eritrea
- Bosnia
- Albania
- Bulgaria
- Romania
- Moldova
- Ukraine
- Belarus
- Kosovo
- Transnistria

Hope & Homes for Children

SOUTH AFRICA

Contents

Mark was educated at the Leys School in Cambridge, commissioned into the 10th Gurkha Rifles in 1962 and went out to Malaya to join his battalion. He saw active service in the jungles of Borneo and Sarawak during the three-year confrontation with the Indonesians. From there he served in Hong Kong, Germany and the UK and commanded his battalion on operations in Belize. He met Caroline while on leave from Malaya in 1965 and they married in 1967. His final posting was as Commander of the first British Contingent in the United Nations Protection Force at the start of the Balkans War in 1992. He retired from the Army early with the rank of Colonel in order to keep the promise he had made to 60 children in Croatia to rebuild their orphanage which had been destroyed by enemy shelling. He and Caroline raised £1 million and successfully completed the project for which he was awarded the OBE.

Caroline was educated at Downe House School near Newbury, Berkshire and then trained as a nursery nurse at Princess Christian College in Windsor. On qualifying as an NNEB nanny she had many happy jobs looking after children in the UK and abroad. After her marriage to Mark she flew out to join him in Hong Kong and over the next 25 years she accompanied him on various postings around the world, moving house 17 times in five different countries. They finally settled in England in 1989. Caroline was awarded the OBE in 2006 for humanitarian services.

In 1994 Mark and Caroline started Hope and Homes for Children, specifically to help orphans of war and disaster. They have appeared on numerous television and radio programmes including *This Is Your Life, Midweek, Hardtalk, How do they do that?, Richard and Judy, Hearts of Gold, Against All Odds and Personality of the Week* on ABC News.

They are now the Founder Presidents of Hope and Homes for Children. They have two children, Edward and William, and four grandchildren, Amelia, Isabelle, Sebastian and Harry.

≈

Those of us who visited or worked in what was Yugoslavia in the early 1990s and especially those who went to Bosnia-Herzogovina and particularly Sarajevo, saw the ravages of war. A civil war is perhaps the most cruel and unpleasant of conflicts. The consequences are felt by everyone - neighbours against neighbours, families divided, children abandoned or worse still orphaned. There is no-one to help. Normal life has ceased. Saddened and horrified by what we saw we went about our business. There were, however, two people who did do something about it. Mark Cook who had been Commander of the British UN Forces in the Balkans, and his wife Caroline, decided that they had to try to help the children who had been abandoned, orphaned or confined in dreadful conditions in orphanages. Although they had no experience of running a charity or organising such an enterprise abroad, they started Hope and Homes for Children. How they managed it I do not know - except that they are two remarkable people who were determined to do what they could to help loveless children.

As you read the book and go from Sierra Leone to Romania, Sudan to Belarus to Eritrea you, too, may well wonder how they did it. Eighty million pounds is a tidy sum to have raised. Thanks to the dedication of two people, who made this commitment to the children, many other people were inspired to support them.

Nobody really knows exactly how many children have benefited from the work of Hope and Homes for Children, but it must be many thousands. As Maria Herczog said, "After almost twenty years of experience in developing their successful model, Hope and Homes for Children is having a truly global impact that will benefit millions of children's lives."

I am sure that those of you who read this book will agree that without the Cooks' intervention a great many more children would still be living in very basic institutions today with no-one to love or care about them. And now there is real hope for those who remain - thanks to Hope and Homes for Children.

Carington.

THE RT. HON. THE LORD CARRINGTON KG GCMG CH MC DL

ᴂ

INTRODUCTION

This is not an 'official' history. It is our recollection of some of the events of the last 20 years, particularly the early years. As such, it has not been subjected to the scrutiny of the 'powers that be' in Hope and Homes for Children (HHC) today or funded by the charity. It is very much our story to thank all those countless people who have trusted and supported us over the years.

It would not be possible to write this book without naming some people, just as it would be impossible to name everyone who has helped us. We realise that we run the risk of upsetting some whose names do not feature and if you are one of them, we are extremely sorry! Literally thousands of you have become part of the HHC 'family' as we like to call it, and have contributed in hundreds of different ways.

You will realise very quickly that we had no business plan, little idea and no experience of running a charity. As we look back we feel somewhat embarrassed by how naïve we were. Both of us had had a loving family and a very happy childhood, and we are fortunate enough to have two boys of our own and now four lovely grandchildren. We are very privileged. It was not until we witnessed the suffering of the children whose lives were torn apart during the war in the Balkans in the early 1990s that we really appreciated our good fortune. Our sole motivation then and now was to help such children and give them a chance in life.

From the start we have had an unshakeable belief that if our work was good enough, the money would come to support it and make it possible. This is clearly a rather risky premise on which to start a charity! If we had written a business plan, as many suggested we should, we now realise that the whole idea would have got no further than the paper on which it was written. It was lucky that neither of us had a clue about business plans!

We would like to emphasise that this is our story as we recall the numerous events in many different countries over the last 20 years. Any inaccuracies of fact or detail are due entirely to our poor memories. The first ten years were particularly exciting and this is reflected in the book. These were our 'pioneering' years when we were responding to events and going to many different countries which, in normal circumstances, we would never have dreamed of going to – Albania, Sierra Leone, Kosovo, Moldova, Belarus, Mozambique – to us these were just names on a map. In those ten years we started programmes in 14 countries. Looking back on it we must have been mad! Getting in and out of these countries was often a challenge in itself, particularly those in which conflicts were still going on. At the same time we were travelling around the UK spreading the word about our work and trying to raise funds to enable us to do it. Life was busy – we were running on adrenaline. It was all-consuming and a lot of fun!

Some chapters in the book are shorter than others. Our work for the children in all the countries has always been of equal importance to us, but we have had more 'adventures' in some countries than in others, particularly in the early days.

The last ten years have, for us, been less exciting as programmes in these countries developed, more people joined us and, of necessity, we handed over the reins to others who have considerably more experience and energy. Our role within HHC has changed and is now mainly concentrated on fundraising. Sadly we now have no involvement in the running of the programmes and rarely meet the children we are trying to help. But this, we realise, is the price of progress.

Throughout the book 'we' refers to the two of us, but on a number of occasions the 'we' refers to Mark and another person or to HHC, the organisation.

HOW IT ALL BEGAN

"The greatest poverty in the world is not the lack of food, it is the lack of love."
Mother Teresa

Early in 1994, on his way back to the UK from Croatia, Mark bought a book at the airport entitled *Natasha's Story* by the ITN war correspondent Michael Nicholson. Sarajevo was under siege at the time and when Michael visited the orphanage he was shocked and moved by the plight of the children who he thought had little chance of survival. One of them, a little girl called Natasha, he smuggled into England. When the story broke, he and his family were besieged by the media and condemned by many for getting emotionally involved. This was not something, he was told, that reporters, particularly one of his experience, should do. Michael dedicated his book to *'Natasha and all those children she left behind'*.

Mark immediately started to read the book. Shortly afterwards, he woke up in the middle of the night and found himself sitting upright in bed, receiving a clear message that he had to go and find out what had happened

Natasha, age 21, on her first return visit to Sarajevo

to those other children who Michael had 'left behind'. The next morning, with some trepidation, he told Caroline of this 'Happening in the Night'. Knowing that he was reading the book, her response was immediate, *"I thought you were going to say something like that. If you go I want to go with you!"* Mark was delighted, but not entirely surprised, by her enthusiastic response.

As Sarajevo was still under siege it was not possible to go in or out unless you were a diplomat, an aid worker with a registered NGO, in the media or in the military. Since Mark had already left the Army to rebuild the orphanage in Croatia, he was none of these. We went to see Michael and we met Natasha, who was bouncing happily on the sofa. Mark asked him what had happened to all the other children he had left behind; he said that he didn't know. We explained that we wanted to go and find out, but we needed help to get there. Michael said it was not a problem, and he would get us accredited as ITN correspondents.

A few days later, armed with our ITN ID cards, we flew to Zagreb, went to the UN headquarters and obtained passes to fly in a military aid aeroplane into Sarajevo. At the airport we waited with some excitement for a plane with room to take us and in anticipation of what was to come. The next one available just happened to be an enormous Russian Air Force Antonov. All passengers flying into Sarajevo had to wear helmets and flak jackets as the Serbs occasionally decided to fire at planes flying over the mountains surrounding the airport.

On arrival in Sarajevo the plane parked as close as possible to the 'terminal building' which was a hut surrounded by sandbags, and still wearing our flak jackets and helmets, we were told to make a dash to it. Here we were checked in by the UN military guard and our passports were stamped *'Maybe Airlines – Sarajevo or Bust. Humanitarian Airlift'*. We were put into an armoured personnel carrier and trundled off to the Holiday Inn hotel which was the only known hotel in the city still operating. It was the de facto HQ of the international media, on the main street and very close to the Serbian frontline. This meant that the exposed side of the building was constantly being fired at. Most of the glass had been blown out and the windows were covered in plastic; running water and electricity were spasmodic. Mark had not thought to explain to Caroline that this Holiday Inn hotel was not quite like others and she was rather surprised by the state of the place and the lack of facilities. The corridor leading to our room was strewn with bricks and rubble – the result of Serbian shellfire. She had presumed there would be a swimming pool and had even packed her swimming costume!

Mark had been to Sarajevo many times during the six months he was Commander of the British UN Forces in the Balkans. On one occasion he had gone to meet Martin Bell, the BBC War Correspondent, to ask for his help in raising the £1 million needed to rebuild the orphanage in Croatia. Martin had been at The Leys School with Mark who was hoping that 'the old school tie' connection might encourage him to agree. Mark recalls, all too clearly, what happened next: *"Martin said he would help if he could. True to his word, as we were discussing what he might do, we heard a big battle going on in the city. We jumped into his BBC armour-plated Land Rover which he fondly called Miss Piggy, with the cameraman and the soundman, and headed for the area. When the noise reached its crescendo we got out in a large, empty square to find out what was happening. It soon became clear that there was a big fire fight going on between the Serbs and Moslems and we were in the middle of it. The soundman told Martin that he thought we had become the targets for both. Sure enough, a few minutes later a stick of mortar bombs landed a few yards away and Martin got a stomach-full of shrapnel. As he lay on the ground, he looked up at the camera and said, 'I have been hit. I am alive. I will survive.' What a wonderful sound bite!"*

Having got Martin back to the French Field Hospital, Mark was asked to take his place on the BBC television's *One O'clock News* in 15 minutes' time. Following the comforting bongs of Big Ben, Mark was interviewed live on air from London. He explained that Martin was alive and in the operating theatre and then immediately went on to make an appeal for help to rebuild the orphanage that he had found! This was his first experience of fundraising and, soon after, Martin sent him a wonderful donation of £500 from his hospital bed in London, with a note thanking him for his help.

This visit by the two of us was the first time that Mark had been into the city as a civilian, without the full armoured protection as a member of the UN Forces. He found it fascinating to see the UN from the outside looking in and discovered the continuously noisy rumble of tracked armoured vehicles grinding around the streets extremely aggravating. He could understand why the overbearing presence of peace-keeping forces in a country is not always popular.

Michael Nicholson had given us some contacts in Sarajevo and one of them, Hilmo Bajgoric, came to meet us in the hotel. Hilmo was about our age, spoke perfect English, and worked for the Bosnian Government; he had a wonderful sense of humour despite his terrible personal circumstances. His wife, a doctor, had managed to get out of Sarajevo with their son, but Hilmo had stayed to look after his elderly mother. In the taxi we took off our flak

jackets and pressed them against the right-hand side of the battered old vehicle to protect ourselves from the Serb snipers. At high speed we drove with Hilmo down 'snipers' alley' and then up the hill to the Bjelave Orphanage.

On our arrival we were surrounded by dozens of unkempt, intimidating teenagers who looked like Dickensian urchins. Their gaunt faces told their own story. Aggressively they demanded money, cigarettes, drugs, food and anything else they could think of.

The building was in a terrible state. It had sustained hits from mortars and heavy weapons in its exposed

position on top of one of the city's hills. Again there was no glass left in any of the windows which were covered in sheets of plastic emblazoned with the UN logo. It was bitterly cold outside and even in the freezing winter there was no heating inside. All the wooden floors and doors had been taken up and used as firewood and all the radiators and pipes had been ripped out and sold. About 20 babies were crammed inside the only warm room in the building. A dangerous-looking gas pipe protruding out of the wall produced a small flame which provided only minimal heat – and plenty of potential danger for small children. Little wonder that even hard-bitten journalists had been shocked at the state of the place, a place where children were barely surviving.

Inside we met the Director. There was a long table with a glass top in his office. Underneath the glass were the business cards of all those people and agencies who had been to visit the orphanage. Most of them had promised to help him in some way, he said, but had failed to do so. We explained what we had already done in Croatia and told him that we wanted to rebuild his orphanage. He did not believe us and was neither interested nor impressed by our offer of help.

As Michael had discovered earlier, the situation was desperate and there was no end in sight. None of the children had been to school for two years. Somehow they had managed to survive on the porridge-type food they were given and by becoming very 'artful dodgers'. They stole food and anything else they could lay their hands on. Some of them had been injured when Serb artillery shells had landed in the playground. They existed from day to day on their wits and had little or no hope for the future.

We visited the children every day that week and began to establish a rapport with them and a few members of the staff. Before we left we told the children that we were going to rebuild their home, but it was obvious that they didn't believe us either. However we just wanted to give them some hope to cling on to.

We got a flight out of Sarajevo on a Luftwaffe transport plane. Once again we had to wear our flak jackets and helmets. The German load master then gave each of us a big, bulky pack to put on. Caroline asked what it was and he replied, *"A parachute."* Having put it on, Caroline then asked what she had to do with it and he just replied, *"I jump ... you jump."*

Full of the emotions we had experienced during the visit and the promise we had made to the children, we pondered on what to do next. Mark told his mother of the new commitment we had made and she said, *"Oh darling, you have done it once, you could never do it again."* Such encouragement! A few days later, whilst walking with our lovely golden retriever, Jess, across the water meadows near our house, the next step became clear to us. We decided to start our own charity to provide homes for orphans of war or disaster; we wanted to give them hope, hence Hope and Homes for Children.

Having made this decision we went to see David Grubb, the Chief Executive of Feed the Children (FTC), who we had met in Bosnia-Herzegovina – we felt we needed his advice. He asked us where our office was going to be; we told

The main entrance to our first office!

him we did not need an office, we would work from home. He told us firmly that this was a mistake as we must plan to expand; *"If you don't"*, he said, *"you will not last long."* So, rather reluctantly, we started looking for office space. A local farmer, Chris Andrews, heard about our plan and offered us the top floor of a barn on his farm. We went to look at it; this entailed going up an outside metal fire-escape to get inside. It was an old hay barn with no windows or heating – and no loo, but fortunately there were plenty of bushes outside! Caroline persuaded Mark that it could be made more habitable so we spent the next few weeks painting it ourselves, buying second-hand furniture and a second-hand laptop which neither of us knew how to use!

Condensation ran down the walls so gas fires and dehumidifiers were our next purchases. This became our office and still is today. Over the years as HHC expanded, we have been able to take over other barn buildings on the farm as they became available. Our landlord, Chris, and his wife Beth, were most helpful; so, too, was a local builder, Phil Budden, who with his two sons carried out all the renovations. After ten years we had about 40 people working there … and ten loos! We are very pleased that we heeded David Grubb's advice about setting up an office.

Being in a barn on a farm ten miles outside Salisbury has its advantages, as well as a few disadvantages. One main advantage is that the rent is very low. Over the years numerous visitors have commented that they were pleased that we were not wasting money on smart offices. For us East Clyffe became our second home.

The postman's arrival every morning was always an exciting moment. How many donations would we receive? One day Mark was on his own and decided to put donations in one pile and bills in another. For the first time there were numerous bills, but not one single donation. Having no-one else to talk to, Mark looked up at the beams in the roof and said, *"Hey you. I thought you wanted us to do this. We can't do it on our own, you know."* Immediately the telephone rang. Mark picked it up very gingerly thinking it might be God at the other end. It wasn't! But it was a very kind lady from Scotland called Jean McCormack, who said, *"You remember that my family trust fund gave you £1,000 last year? I thought you would like to know that we have just had a meeting and we have decided to give you £2,000 this year."* Mark thanked her profusely, put down the telephone, looked up and said, *"Okay. You win. Thank you."* We told one lady about this coincidence and she responded immediately saying that it was a 'Godincidence'. We have had many more of these 'Godincidences' since.

On 1 April 1994 Mark received a letter from The Townswomen's Guilds Head Office inviting him to speak at their Annual Conference in the Royal Albert Hall to an audience of 5,000 women, including HRH Princess Anne, their President. We presumed this was an April Fools' joke! It wasn't. Apparently the media coverage of the rebuilding of the orphanage in Croatia had sparked a wide interest.

In his research for the speech Mark discovered that an amazing woman called Eglantyne Jebb had visited Europe after the First World War; she was so moved by the poor children whose lives had been torn apart, that she decided to start a charity which she called Save the Children. On 17 May 1917 she held the inaugural meeting in the Royal Albert Hall. On 29 June 1994 Mark addressed the Townswomen's Guilds conference and announced that, as a consequence of our own experience in the Balkans War, we were going to start a new charity to provide homes for orphans of war or disaster. It was such an extraordinary coincidence, especially since Princess Anne is President of Save the Children.

And so, HHC was launched in the same place – the Royal Albert Hall – as Save the Children had been 77 years earlier. We became a Registered Charity on 31 August 1994 and held a Press Conference to explain our plans in London on 3 October, Universal Children's Day. James Ruddy, the Deputy Editor of the *Eastern Daily Press (EDP)* newspaper, attended the conference. Mark was born in Suffolk in a small town called Beccles, so the editors considered this a 'local boy' story. From this moment on, the newspaper became a great champion of our work and always refers to 'Beccles-born Mark Cook' much to the annoyance of Caroline who was born in Cheltenham, which they never mention! At the end of the press conference James presented us with a cheque from *EDP* readers for the staggering amount of £20,000. This was an amazing surprise and our first really big donation. Now we really felt we were 'in business'.

Shortly afterwards we were contacted by a researcher for a television programme called *How Do They Do That?* who said that they wanted to feature us. A few days later a film crew came down to our office at East Clyffe. We were bemused by the whole idea and couldn't understand why they wanted to film us, to which they replied, *"Don't you think it's rather extraordinary that here you are, in an old barn in the depths of the country, saving the lives of numerous abandoned children in war zones?"* We had never for a moment thought of it as extraordinary. We decided to go along with the idea as it was obviously good advertising! A short film was made and we were invited to the studio where it was shown to a live audience; then we were interviewed by the host of the programme. The response was very exciting and one outcome in particular was to change the course of HHC. The programme showing our work had caught the attention of one young man who was to greatly influence the whole future and focus of the charity.

Within a few days we received a long letter from him; his name was James Whiting. He explained that he didn't really know why he was writing, but just wanted us to know how moved and impressed he was by what we were doing. Caroline responded with an equally long letter to which James replied, telling us more about himself. He was 28, a qualified lawyer, and working for a big London law firm. During his gap year he had worked as a volunteer in a school for disabled children in Umtata, South Africa, before going to Durham University. While at university, after a few beers with a friend one Sunday lunchtime, the two of them decided to cycle from London to Umtata at the end of their degree course in order to raise money for the school. Obviously they'd had a few too many beers! But they did it – at least James did. His friend decided to go back home when they were cycling along a railway line in the Nubian desert in Sudan. Undaunted, James cycled on alone.

Soon after he joined the law firm he was briefed to meet a lady seeking legal advice about her divorce. Being new to the job, James was very nervous about doing this, but had no option. On arrival at her hotel he found a very distraught woman, sobbing, with her head in her hands. Eventually she looked up and he realised it was Esther Rantzen and he became extremely flustered! The whole scene was being filmed by hidden cameras and Esther was acting the role. He had been ambushed by Esther Rantzen's programme called *Hearts of Gold*. Coincidentally we had also been ambushed by her for the same programme in 1993 when we were rebuilding the orphanage in Croatia.

Immediately after meeting Esther, James was flown out to South Africa and taken back to Umtata. He received a wonderful greeting from Sister Mary Paule (who ran the school), the staff, the children and James were all filmed. The programme was shown on television a little later. Following James's letter, his mother, Rosemary, sent us a video of the programme which we immediately sat down to watch. We were only half way through when we turned it off, looked at each other, and decided that we just had to meet James. Shortly afterwards we did so and straightaway realised that he was such a special person we really wanted him to work with us. We asked him if he would consider doing so. Without hesitating he said, *"Yes!"* Then we had to explain to him that we had very limited funds, that we could not afford to pay him much – nothing like the amount he was currently earning. He said, *"I'm not in it for the money"*

James and Mark in the office

and the next day he handed in his notice to his law firm so that he could join us.

On 10 October 1996 James was due to arrive at 9am. We were very excited. We had bought him a second-hand desk and chair, but his computer was brand new; we presumed that this would be of the greatest importance to him. We waited and waited; at 10.30am we decided that he'd obviously changed his mind. Then we heard spluttering. Looking down from the top of our barn's fire escape steps, we saw a very old car with a broken exhaust pipe. James got out of the car, looked up at us, put his finger in his mouth like a naughty boy, smiled and apologised for being late. This was not the start we had expected, but we were so relieved to see him that we forgave him immediately. About a month later James asked us if we knew how to turn on his computer!

Right from the start James was as passionate about our work as we were; he was totally committed and incredibly hard-working. However, being a very bright, young lawyer he started asking awkward questions, querying what we were doing and how we were doing it. Mark became the archetypal grumpy old colonel and rather resented this questioning approach! Caroline and James schemed behind his back when he was out (on most evenings he was giving Rotary Club talks) discussing ideas and how to get Mark to see sense. Mark's big plan at the time was to create a worldwide network of small, well-run orphanages, building two new ones each year, with a 'mother home' in the UK which, he planned, would probably be in an old,

James in Sierra Leone

disused boarding school, with large grounds and a lake. His idea was that the children from the various orphanages around the world would come there for a few weeks at a time, learn English, have lots of fun and get to know children in other HHC homes around the world. Caroline and James thought it was a crazy idea and developed various subtle tactics to get Mark to change his mind about this and some of his other odd ideas.

Caroline would often say to Mark, the morning after he'd been giving a talk somewhere, *"James and I were discussing things last night when you were out and we're wondering whether we should do something slightly different."* Mark would go off in a huff, think about it for a few days and then tell James he had had a good idea. He would feed back James's idea as if it was his own! This amused Caroline but made James rather angry.

Some time later James suggested that we should make the homes as small as possible with perhaps only five or six children in each, then they would feel more like a typical family. Caroline agreed, but Mark initially did not, saying that this would be far too expensive and prevent us from helping many more children as quickly as possible. James's response was that we had never asked the children what they wanted and perhaps we should. So that is exactly what we did. On our visits to all the countries we were then working in, we made a point of asking the children what they really wanted. It did not matter what race, colour or creed they were, or whether they were living in an orphanage, on the streets or in the sewers, their answer was always the same, *"Please, please find me a family, I want a home."* Mark asked one small boy on the streets of Khartoum what he thought a family and a home were and his response was *"Love"*. That response was to have a defining influence on the future focus of HHC. Previously we had rather presumed that the most important things that these vulnerable children needed were food, a roof over their heads, a safe place to sleep and an education. But the children themselves guided us to the heart of our mission – they desperately wanted and needed to be loved.

Over the years we have visited numerous orphanages in many countries. Some were so awful and smelly that we immediately felt sick and wanted to leave; others were better, being reasonably well-equipped and staffed. But the one thing we never found in any orphanage was the feeling of unconditional love that is at the heart of a caring family.

Love became the key to our work and we have quite unashamedly focussed on and talked about it ever since. And it was James who started us on this journey of discovery. We, and the children, owe him so much.

❧

WELCOME TO SARAJEVO
BOSNIA-HERZEGOVINA

1994 -

The Situation: From 1992 to 1995 a vicious war raged between the Croatians, Muslims and Serbs.

The Problem: Families were displaced and torn apart, leaving countless orphaned and vulnerable children.

Our Initial Plan: To repair the damaged orphanage in Sarajevo.

The Outcome: We rebuilt the orphanage and continue to work in the country reforming the childcare system.

"The orphanage is the worst place in Sarajevo aside from the morgue."
Janine di Giovanni in *The Times*

Oggi Tomic taken by his friend and mentor Chris Leslie

Getting into Sarajevo was always a challenge … and exciting. And once in, you never knew how, when or even if you would ever get out. Serb gunners in the surrounding hills fired onto the streets for four years, killing 10,000 men, women and children. You could turn a corner and attract a sniper's bullet immediately. Or you might venture across a junction and be torn to pieces by white-hot shrapnel from a mortar blast. Life was merely about survival – finding food, water and a place to sleep, just for another day, another night. Few people could look much further ahead.

The 'best' way to get into the besieged city was by air. But sometimes the airport, this key link with the outside world, was closed for weeks as the Serbs said they would fire missiles at any aircraft approaching and, to prove their point, shot down an Italian plane taking in aid, killing the four crew members. All the houses near the airport terminal were badly damaged by shell fire and most people had left the area. The city streets were empty of all life, except for occasional figures scurrying to safety and heavily-armoured UN vehicles growling along. On the side of the road there was a big sign pockmarked by bullets and shrapnel saying, ironically, 'Welcome to Sarajevo!'

Without technical experience we were clueless about how difficult it would be to repair the city's shattered Bjelave Orphanage and how much it might cost, so we sought the help of a great friend. Bill Dawson had served in the Gurkhas with Mark for 30 years and was now working for Wimpey, the construction company. We asked him if he could arrange for a suitable quantity surveyor to go out with us to assess the project. A few days later we received a very hesitant

telephone call from a man called Ken Groves who said he was a senior surveyor at Wimpey. He had asked for volunteers, but none had come forward; *"So"*, he said, *"I suppose I will have to go to Sarajevo with you myself."* Two weeks later we flew back to Sarajevo with Ken who was extremely helpful and gave us a good idea of what was required and how much it might cost … a mere £400,000!

Ken Groves with some children in Wimpey T shirts

Ken agreed to be one of our first Trustees and has been a stalwart supporter of HHC ever since.

The next step was to find a builder to carry out the reconstruction of the orphanage, so we put an advertisement in the local newspaper, *Oslobođenje*, which miraculously had been produced every day during the siege. Four bids came in and soon Mark flew out to interview the contenders with Hilmo, our local adviser. One was a very big firm which constructed huge projects abroad. We went to see Mr Big in his big office and asked him if he had been to the orphanage himself. He said that he had not, but that he had sent one of his men. We got up and said *"Goodbye"*; he was very surprised.

The last firm Mark and Hilmo met was a Bosnian husband and wife team, Osman and Vesna Halebic. Osman was a builder/carpenter and Vesna an experienced architect; they had two teenage sons. Previously they had lived in their own very nice house near the airport in an area called Ilija, but the Serbs came and gave them two hours to get out during which time they frantically dug a big hole in their garden and buried their precious possessions. Now they were squatting in a small, exposed and very dangerous, top storey flat which had belonged to a Serb who had left Sarajevo. We asked them if they had been to the orphanage. They laughed, saying they had spent a week there with their sons measuring every inch of the place, then invited us to ask any questions about it. They impressed us with their knowledge and genuine sincerity. What an incredible find they were.

Vesna and Osman with their sons and Mark

The next day we went back to meet Osman and Vesna and told them we would give them the contract. They were overcome with emotion; we had given them a chance to rebuild their own lives and they promised not to let us down. There was only one problem – they had no money, had lost all their equipment to the Serbs and had to lay off their workforce. Very shyly, they asked if we could give them some cash to get started. Money was a huge problem in Sarajevo during the siege as all the banks were closed, and cash was required for everything. The German Deutschmark (DM) was preferred to any other currency but only in small denomination notes. Fortunately, in anticipation, we had taken some cash in with us. Much to their surprise we said we trusted them and gave them DM 10,000. Again, they were completely overwhelmed by this. We signed a contract with them for the rebuilding of the home on 10 April 1995.

Osman and Vesna were true to their word and did a remarkable job in completing the work to a very high standard in nine months. The task was immensely difficult because of the scarcity of building materials in the city; much of it had to be pulled through a tunnel which had been dug under the airport runway. Realising we needed a huge amount of cash to complete the project, and hoping he might be able to help us, Mark went to meet the British Ambassador to ask how we could get money into the city. He told us that the only way was to bring it in ourselves; this was not the response we wanted!

This was a daunting prospect. We would have to carry large amounts of cash into the city, where many people were armed and so desperate that they would do almost anything to survive. To make matters worse, the Serbs were regularly closing the airport by threatening to shoot down planes. The only other way in was over the infamous Mount Igman track which was under fire in places from Serb artillery and heavy machine guns. On one occasion, six people were killed on the mountain in two separate attacks while Mark was in the country. But there was no other option and occasionally we had to make the trip. The risks were worthwhile and necessary, in order to keep the construction work going.

Once, Mark went into the city over the mountain road carrying a huge pile of German DM, worth about £75,000 in cash. The small denomination DM notes were stored in two money belts worn under his Barbour jacket. He looked like the Michelin man! Today's Trustees would have been horrified at our taking such a colossal risk, but our Trustees at the time – Michael Nicholson (Chairman), Ken Groves and a long-term friend, Deirdre Green – were not as 'hands on' as are today's Trustees. In fact it had not even occurred to us to inform them of what we were doing!

On returning home after one such journey, Mark wrote in a report, '*Just before we entered the most dangerous section of the mountain road, we were stopped at a checkpoint jointly manned by Bosnian and UN soldiers. Our confidence was not helped by a lengthy argument between them as to whether it was safe to proceed. The Bosnian waved us on urgently, but a French soldier stood resolutely in the middle of the road saying "Non". Eventually, our impatience to press on won the day and we arrived in a totally dark city just 15 minutes before the curfew. We had been on the road for over 12 hours and I went straight to Osman and Vesna's house. We talked late into the night about what had happened since my last visit, drinking the whisky which I had taken for them.*

'*I was delighted to see the progress that the builders had made since my last visit and the home is now over half-finished. This is a remarkable achievement considering the particularly bad shelling to which Sarajevo has been subjected and the difficulties of getting building materials. Much of what was not available in the city itself has to be brought in through the tiny tunnel which, apart from humanitarian aid, has been the umbilical cord keeping the people alive since the siege started three years ago.*'

Around this time we were contacted by ABC News, the well-known American television company. They wanted to make Mark their '*Personality of the Week*' in the near future and to film him in Sarajevo. The call came out of the blue; we had no idea how they had heard about us and our work.

A few weeks later Mark flew to Split on the Croatian coast and met the producer and film crew from the USA. The airport was closed so they hired an old, armour-plated Land Rover for the journey into Sarajevo over Mount Igman once again. After a few days of filming in the city and in the orphanage, discussions took place as to the safest time to leave, using the Mount Igman route. When would the Serbs be least alert? As always everyone had their own theories on this, but it was decided that early in the morning would be the best bet – and it really was like making a pretty big bet. The stakes were high. This was akin to Russian roulette.

The following morning Mark and the television crew set off early. The Land Rover was packed with people and equipment and Mark squeezed into the back. With its heavy armour plating and being grossly overloaded, progress up Mount Igman was painfully slow.

Mark wrote later, '*Apart from the straining of the engine there was deathly silence from everyone as we entered the 'killing zone' of open ground. Suddenly, there was an enormous bang as the back door burst open and equipment fell out and started rolling down the hill. We had no option but to stop – in full view of the Serb gunners – and retrieve everything, finally packing it back into the vehicle. It only took about five minutes, but it seemed a great deal longer. The back door latch was faulty and we had to hold it shut as the vehicle continued slowly up the hill. Thankfully the Serb gunners must have had a good time the night before; they had a reputation of being very heavy drinkers and they were probably suffering the consequences.*'

Such dangers were only part of the rebuilding project. There were also some unbelievably frustrating hurdles to cross. The Bjelave Orphanage had two buildings; a large, old house which belonged to the Roman Catholic Church and a much bigger, modern, purpose-built orphanage which belonged to the Government. Since the Church decided they wanted their building back we carried out the reconstruction of the larger building. Behind these two buildings was a piece of land which, we thought, could be used as a play area by all the children in the neighbourhood. We invited an architect to design a playground and arranged a meeting to discuss this with the Bishop of Sarajevo. Sadly he did not agree with the idea on the grounds that the Christian children who would use their building were different from the Muslim children in the orphanage. He suggested that either each group should have set times when they could use it or they could put up a fence to segregate the children. We were shocked and dismayed by his attitude and said so. Shortly afterwards a ten foot wire mesh fence was erected by the Church to keep the children apart.

Finally, though, the building project was completed. It was a great relief and we were eager to celebrate it with the children themselves so, in December 1995, just after the Dayton Peace Agreement was signed, we went to Sarajevo with William, our

With William en route to Sarajevo in 1995

younger son, and James Ruddy. We wanted to see the children and organise a Christmas party for them as a special treat. Since the orphanage staff were not the slightest bit interested in helping us we organised it ourselves, buying anything we could from the shops in Sarajevo which were still not well stocked. Despite this we managed to find enough sweets, drinks, balloons and toys that children like and arranged tables and chairs for all of them in the main hall where we created a wonderful atmosphere. For the older ones it was the first party they had been to for four years and for the younger ones, their first ever. We think they all enjoyed it, we certainly did.

Whilst in the city we stayed in an apartment belonging to a very kind Bosnian Muslim family who lived on the floor below. As there was no running water at the time in Sarajevo, they had to collect the water they needed from standpipes. During the siege this was very dangerous since long queues of people formed outside in the open where they were vulnerable to shell, mortar and sniper fire. Our host family had very thoughtfully filled up many large plastic bottles of water for our use and placed them in the kitchen. Caroline got up early on the first morning to make tea for the four of us as we got dressed. After a few minutes we all became aware of a strong, pungent smell. We could not think what it was until we suddenly realised that it was coming from the kettle. Amongst the bottles of water, they had put a few litre bottles of slivovitz, which is a clear plum brandy – a vital necessity for most Bosnians, particularly in a war zone. Caroline had unknowingly poured a bottle of slivovitz into the kettle and it was now merrily bubbling away, being distilled for the second time!

On one of Mark's previous visits to Sarajevo, James Ruddy, who wanted to write a feature for his newspaper, had gone with him and they had stayed with the same Muslim family. There was a curfew at the time which prohibited movement after dark, but as we had no food we decided to chance our luck and go to an underground café that we had been told about. It was 15 minutes' walk away. We ordered the very basic highly-questionable burgers that they had – and some beer which somehow was always available. Shortly afterwards there was an enormous explosion as an artillery shell landed very close-by. Seconds later the door flew open and two teenage boys crashed into the café in a state of shock. They had had a very narrow escape. We soon made friends and they joined us for dinner. After they had calmed down a bit, we had an interesting talk with them about their lives, the situation and their hopes for the future. Eventually we crept back to the house in the dark. We were very relieved to have survived this unusual evening and, thankfully, James produced a bottle of duty-free whisky to celebrate. Mark swears that James drank most of it!

The next morning it was obvious that James had a bad hangover but, undaunted, he was determined to go and interview the Bosnian leader, President Izetbegović. His office in the Presidency was very heavily guarded by big men and surrounded by sandbags. Mark went with James and stopped when they were about 200 yards away. He watched anxiously as James began to weave his way towards the building. James showed the guards his Press pass and told them he had an appointment to interview the President. Somehow he managed to bluff his way into the President's outer office. Here he was confronted by more heavily-armed men who asked him who he was and what he was doing there. He explained, in his distinctive North country accent, that he was the Deputy Editor of the famous award-winning *Eastern Daily Press* newspaper, based in Norwich in Norfolk, England, and that he had come out specifically to meet the President. His luck ran out. They were not impressed and he was speedily escorted out of the building.

Moments of joy and high humour were important in keeping us all sane. But we were brought down to earth by the daily realities and frustrations at the newly-built orphanage. One day when we were talking to the Director, a tall, thin, anxious-looking teenage girl came up to us and butted into our conversation, trying to attract our attention. Slightly surprised by this abrupt interruption, we told her that we were busy at that moment and did not have time to talk to her. She stood her ground and said, slightly aggressively, *"That's the trouble, no-one ever has time for me."* We felt very guilty and her response went straight to our hearts. Standing in the entrance hall later that day we watched as a group of young children from the orphanage carrying small backpacks were returning from their primary school. Out of curiosity we stopped one small boy and asked him to show us what was inside his pack. He squatted down and began to chat away enthusiastically. With great pride he showed us all the ticks in his work books, one after another. Although, sadly, we could not understand what he was saying, the message was very clear. He was excited that, at last, someone was taking an interest in him as an individual. Whenever we went into a room where there were little children, they always lifted up their arms wanting to be hugged. The only physical contact they ever had was when they were changed and occasionally sluiced down, often in cold water. They longed to be cuddled. We were both horrified at the barren emptiness of their young lives. A tearful Caroline summed it up: *"We can't let these children carry on like this; it's heart-breaking. All they want are hugs and lots of love."*

We decided that we should arrange for volunteers from the UK to go out to help in the orphanage for a few months at a time, and give the children their time and love. The first two - Sarah and Peter - had to face the challenge of not being accepted by the staff in the home, some of whom resented their presence and could see no reason for it. Being young and enthusiastic they soon forged a bond with all the children by talking and listening to the older ones and playing with the younger ones. (Peter later went on to be one of our volunteers in Sierra Leone.) When they left, the teenagers in the home gave them a remarkable letter thanking them for their love. Considering the lives they had led and their suffering, it was very telling that they should write such a letter unashamedly talking about the love they felt – possibly for the first time in their lives. Over the next few years several more people went out as volunteers. One of the first was Julia Downe, an occupational therapist who was working in Salisbury, and in 1997 she became our first Country Director.

We suspected that the majority of the children in the institution were not actually orphans. We discovered that some had living relatives who occasionally came to visit them, often much to the embarrassment of the children themselves.

But the Director would not let us see the children's records, so we were unable to find out much about them apart from what they told us. After the peace agreement, UNICEF arranged a meeting in Sarajevo for all the leading children's agencies working in the country. Mark attended with the Director. No-one knew how many children were being looked after in all the various types of institutions in the country, so it was decided that it would be a good idea to carry out a survey of all the children and document their personal details. Everyone agreed that this was necessary and that the obvious place to start would be the Bjelave Orphanage in Sarajevo. Before closing the meeting, the Chairman went round the table asking if there were any additional points anyone wanted to raise. Sitting next to the Director Mark heard him say in a low, clear voice, *"No-one is going to come into my orphanage because I run the best orphanage in the world."* The audit never happened.

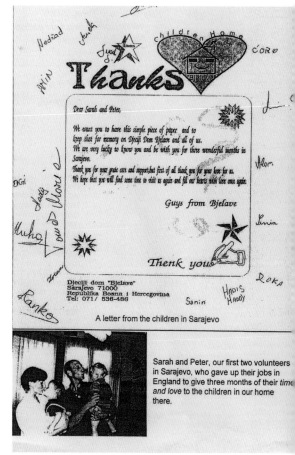

A letter from the children in Sarajevo

Sarah and Peter, our first two volunteers in Sarajevo, who gave up their jobs in England to give three months of their *time and love* to the children in our home there.

Oggi Tomic was the youngest of the teenagers in the home and, as such, he was picked on and bullied by some of the older boys. They made him run errands and get food and cigarettes for them. Oggi, like all the others in the orphanage, became a very accomplished thief; they worked in teams using diversionary tactics which helped them steal food from market stalls.

Chris Leslie, a university student in Glasgow, went out to Sarajevo in his vacations four years running to teach photography to any of the teenagers in the orphanage who were interested. Oggi showed a great interest and a natural aptitude and he soon became a very proficient photographer. This was to change his life in the most remarkable way.

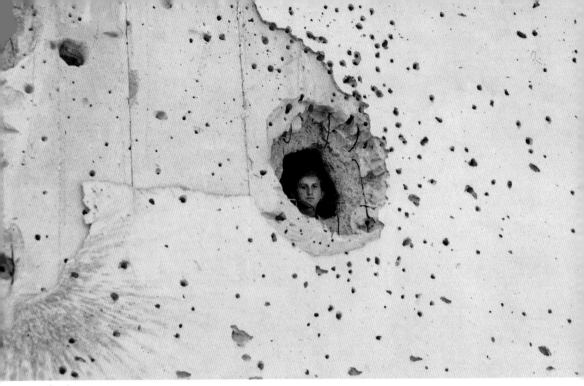

Oggi

Recognising Oggi's determination to make something of his life, we arranged for him to come to the UK two years running to attend a summer school for foreign children. It was run by the Cambridge Language and Activities Centre (CLAC) who kindly gave us two free places each year. Oggi so impressed the staff that he was invited back year after year to help run the course. He saved all his earnings from CLAC and undertook various photography jobs in Sarajevo. A very determined young man, he succeeded in gaining a place at the University of Wales, Newport, where he undertook a three-year degree course in documentary film making. He graduated at the same time as Alexandra Smart, our book cover photographer. In 2012 Oggi, with his good friend and mentor Chris Leslie, went back to Bosnia to try and find his family and discover why he had been abandoned at birth and put in an orphanage. They made an extraordinarily moving and powerful one-hour documentary film called *Finding Family* – Oggi's journey back into his past. It has won many awards, including two BAFTAs. We attended the premier

Oggi and Chris Leslie

which was in Sarajevo, and it has been shown at many cinemas abroad and also in the UK, thanks to Tim Richards, our current Chairman of Trustees who is also the Founder and CEO of Vue Cinemas.

Oggi with good friends at his graduation

Oggi, now happily married to Aggie from Poland, lives in Cambridge. He is our greatest global ambassador and a vociferous spokesman against institutionalised care. His success is a wonderful example of what can be achieved when we are able to unlock the potential in vulnerable children.

For many years Julia Downe tried to help the Director understand that institutionalised care of children was not in their best interests and that HHC would like to support him and work with the authorities in Sarajevo in reforming their childcare system. We brought him to the UK on several occasions to meet our other country representatives to share experiences and hear from experts in the field. But for him, the institution provided a good job as it did for his staff and he was determined to keep the status quo. Meanwhile, Julia worked tirelessly with the children to help them improve their lives in any way she could. She also enabled some of the older children to leave the home by finding them jobs and somewhere to live. Several years later Julia married a compassionate Bosnian lawyer, Zanid Kragulj, and they now have two young sons and live in Sarajevo.

Our work progressed and in January 2001 we opened our first Mother and Baby Unit in the country, in the orphanage building. Anna, the first mother to benefit from it, sent an open letter to all young mothers like herself who found themselves in such a critical situation, urging them not to give up their children to the orphanage. She wrote, *'Dear Mothers. Don't let anybody else take care of your child. The person that child needs is you. Don't abandon your child.'* We were present when another teenager, who had been forced by her family to put her new-born baby in the orphanage, was admitted to the Mother and Baby Unit and reunited with her baby for the first time. As the nurse put the little girl in her mother's arms, we were all overcome with emotion.

Joan from Norfolk with 'her family' oustide their home in Zenica

The family's shack in the mountains

The family and their new house in the mountains under construction

Our work was becoming well known across the country and the Director of a children's home in Zenica asked for our help. She wanted to close it down, despite the fact that it was a really nice building and much more homely than most institutions. There were 90 children in it. We managed to reunite the majority of them with their families, but for 12 children, this was not possible at the time, and one very special lady in Norfolk funded a small home for them. Three of these children, who were siblings, did have parents who desperately wanted to look after them, but were too poor to do so. They survived on subsistence farming and lived in a shack high up in the mountains above Zenica in a beautiful but remote area. The parents loved their children and the children desperately wanted to go back and live with them. Fortunately the same kind lady who funded the home in Zenica also generously funded another home for this family. On seeing the success of this closure the authorities in other Cantons asked for our help in developing care services for their children.

As it was clear that the Director of the Bjelave Orphanage was never going to change his mind about the need for deinstitutionalisation (DI) we decided to withdraw our support for his institution in 2006. Instead we concentrated our efforts on supporting vulnerable families – and there were far too many of them – so that they were not forced to send their children to an orphanage in the first place. We started to work with the local authorities, training their staff on preventing the separation of children from parents, and helping to reform their childcare system.

Shortly after we withdrew our support from the orphanage, a fire broke out one night in the nursery. Only one member of staff was on duty at the time. Sadly she was unable to rescue all of the children and six of them died from smoke inhalation. The Director and the system were never held to account. The final straw for us came when we heard that a little girl in the orphanage who we knew, aged about four, who constantly hit her head with both her hands through sheer frustration, became blind. She was transferred to yet another orphanage – one for blind children. We wrote a strong letter to the Director, asking him if he could now see the terrible consequences of institutionalised care. He did not reply.

Julia, who is now our Regional Childcare Adviser for Europe, told us recently about a specific memory that has had a lasting impact on her. She wrote, '*In the early days when I was working as a volunteer in the orphanage in Sarajevo, there was one little boy, about three years old, who took a particular shine to me. He would come to me every day, wanting to be held and cuddled, and I cuddled him as much as I could. But it broke my heart that I couldn't give him what he really*

Julia Downe

wanted from me: he wanted me to love him more than I loved the other children, to single him out as my favourite. Of course I couldn't give that kind of exclusive love without being unfair to all the other children. This is what convinced me that simply improving institutions can never give children what they really need – the exclusive love and attachment of a parent or carer and the feeling of belonging to a family.'

Jasna (right) signing a Memorandum of Understanding (MOU) on DI in Neretva Canton

Anisija

Although it is now 19 years since the end of the Balkans War, Bosnia Herzegovina is still recovering from that devastating conflict. Unemployment is extremely high and there are still countless families who are displaced and struggling to survive. As we have experienced in other countries, it takes a very long time and much patience to rebuild a fractured society where the poorest are the most vulnerable.

Across this small and impoverished country, there are still about 2,000 children hidden away in bleak, State-run institutions. Although the Government has made a commitment to replace these with alternative family-based care systems, it still lacks the specialist skills needed to develop the new systems and the financial resources to develop them speedily.

Our small, dedicated team, led by Anisija Radenkovic and Jasna Hodzic, is now working in partnership with UNICEF and the Bosnian Government to reform the country's child protection system. Our aim is to prevent children under the age of five from being placed in institutions, to have fewer school age children in residential care and to bring the country closer to eradicating institutional care for children altogether. To achieve this, we are developing long-term programmes to support vulnerable children and their families and creating services to help children move into, or remain in, loving family environments.

ﻋ

FLEEING FROM THE REBELS
SIERRA LEONE

GUINEA
Kamakwie

Makeni

Lungi Airport

Freetown

SIERRA LEONE

Bo

LIBERIA

Atlantic Ocean

1996 - 2013

The Situation: There was a brutal civil war from 1991 to 2002.

The Problem: Countless children were orphaned and displaced from their homes.

Our Initial Plan: To provide a home for 40 orphaned children whom we found in displaced persons' camps in Freetown.

The Outcome: We built four homes and then expanded our programme, helping hundreds of children and families. In 2013 we handed over our programme to a local NGO.

"Shooting somebody became like drinking a glass of water."
Ishmael Beah, a former child soldier in Sierra Leone

Inside one of the displaced camps

I went into the smoky, dark, smelly, disused brick factory which was now 'home' for about 5,000 people, crammed in with barely room to move between the bodies lying on the floor. One woman had just died and was being washed; there was no privacy or dignity, even in death. In the middle of this charnel house I met Mauwinnie. I bent down, took her hands and we just looked at each other, in silence. What can you possibly say to a frightened little girl who has suffered so cruelly? I smiled and she smiled and we were friends – for life. As I was shown round the camp, followed by numerous inquisitive children, Mauwinnie clung to my hand. I am positive she sensed 'hope'. Eventually we had to leave. I told her I would be back, unlocked her hand and got into the truck. As we drove away I turned and saw she was staring at me. I wondered what she was thinking. Does she really believe I will return? She has to, because she only has 'hope' to cling on to now. I knew we had to go back. (Mark)

From the start of HHC we felt uneasy about only helping the children in Bosnia-Herzegovina. We had already declared our mission … *'To give hope to orphans of war and disaster'* … and since there were numerous conflicts going on in Africa, as well as the terrible pandemic of HIV / AIDS, we were anxious to do something there. But where? The choice was too great.

And then, early in 1995, the choice was made for us. Caroline was busy in the kitchen at home when the telephone rang and the operator asked her if she would accept a reverse charge call from Sierra Leone. As she did not know anyone in Sierra Leone (or exactly where it was!), Caroline was so intrigued that she agreed and the voice at the other end asked her if HHC provided homes for orphans of war. Rather diffidently Caroline said, *"Yes"* and the caller went on to explain that there was a war going on in Sierra Leone and he asked if we could help his small organisation which comprised a group of Baptist school teachers who wanted to help the orphaned children. Caroline took his telephone number – it was, unbelievably, a mobile! – saying she would discuss it with Mark when he got back from Sarajevo in a few days' time.

On Mark's return our first job was to identify Sierra Leone on the map! Then we called the number. Peter Lamin, who had made the first telephone call, explained that the organisation was called HANCi, standing for Help A Needy Child International. It seemed a rather pretentious title for such a small organisation. He said they wanted to help the children who had lost their homes and families in the terrible civil war that was still going on in the country. This was just the kind of invitation we had been looking for, so we decided to go out to Sierra Leone to see how we could help. We were intrigued to know how they had heard of us and Peter explained that a Dr. James had told them. To this day we do not know who Dr. James was, but we have much to thank him for, and so do hundreds of children in Sierra Leone. We explained that we were a very small organisation with very little money and Mark told them he would go out, but on no account were they to put him in a smart, expensive hotel. Little did he know that there were very few hotels still operating in Sierra Leone – and certainly none of them was smart!

Having obtained a visa, Mark flew out two weeks later arriving late one night and was greeted by a group of smiling men in a battered old pick-up truck. The airport building was unlike any he had ever seen. Outside it was pitch dark – there was no electricity anywhere. They drove to the ferry a few miles away to take them across to the mainland. After two hours drinking warm beer in a shack, an ancient ferry arrived. Pushing and shouting, hundreds of people literally piled on to the boat to cross into Freetown, the capital. Mark could not see any land or lights ahead and after some time felt rather anxious until it was explained to him that there was no electricity in Freetown either. On arrival he was taken to the YMCA in a run-down part of the city. He was told to lock his door and make sure he did not open it until they came

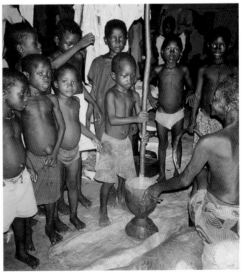

A white circle marked a family's living space

44

to collect him the next morning. The night was hot, the room stuffy and Mark was woken frequently by strange noises. The following day he was taken around the displaced persons' camps where thousands of people were crammed together in large, old, derelict factories and warehouses. Chalk circles on the floor denoted the living space of each family. In amongst this seething mass of sad, destitute people were some children who had no known relatives to look after them – Mauwinnie was one of them.

Hope Bear helping a little girl in a refugee camp

The country was caught in a wild and unpredictable war in which bands of drug-crazed rebel fighters were marauding en masse. The main group, the Revolutionary United Front, had committed countless atrocities: slaughtering whole villages and hacking off arms and legs in a campaign designed to cause abject terror. Hollywood's *Blood Diamond* film loosely portrays the madness and some of the causes, including the exchange of a limitless supply of weapons for some of the country's easily excavated alluvial diamonds. This access to instant wealth had turned the world's poorest country into a surreal funfair for the wicked and a nightmare for the innocent.

A little girl whose arm was chopped off by the rebels

Before the war the population of Freetown had been a million and even then the old sewage system could not cope. Now, every day more and more displaced persons were arriving and the number had gone up to over three million people, the majority of whom had fled in fear to the city for safety. As a result there was now a serious problem with sanitation, causing many health issues from overflowing open drains and sewers. In Freetown, Mark witnessed a teeming anthill of a city. Streets were piled with sewage and filth; people were walking round in rags and there was chaos and confusion everywhere. A frenzy of uncertainty and panic filled the air, as the so called peace-keeping forces sent from other African countries were known to melt away at the first sign of combat with the rebels.

Dr. Roland Kargbo

Mark was driven through the crazily-crammed streets to Dr. Roland Kargbo's office in the centre of Freetown to discuss various ideas and options with him. He was the Director of Education for the 26 Baptist schools and a Vocational Institute in the country. Roland and his family had spent six years in Germany where he was sponsored by the Baptist Ministry to study for a doctorate in Educational Planning. He was like a breath of fresh air and Mark was immediately struck by his calm nature, his modesty, sincerity and a genuine desire to help children who had lost their families and homes. Roland wanted to create a safe haven for those children who had been orphaned.

International adoption became a contentious issue when we learned that HANCi had a partnership with an American adoption agency. We had heard allegations that some very poor families who were being paid to give their children up for adoption, then realised that this was a good way of making money, so they began to produce yet more children with the intention of selling them for cash. The only dispute we ever had with Roland was when we told him that we could not work with his organisation if he continued to send small children to the USA. Roland said, *"Are you telling me that these vulnerable children are better off here in Sierra Leone than they would be in the USA?"* After a lively discussion he eventually agreed to have nothing more to do with international adoption, but would concentrate on helping vulnerable children to grow up in their home country, Sierra Leone.

Because of the fear, chaos and tension in Freetown, Roland suggested that it would be better and safer to create a home for the children in Makeni, the second biggest town in Sierra Leone, about 75 miles north east of Freetown. He knew the Paramount Chief who, he said, was a good and trustworthy man who would be willing to help us. Mark said he would like to go there the next day and Roland agreed to provide his own truck and driver to take him. Later that evening Mark went to have a drink with the British High Commissioner and told him of his plan saying, *"I am not asking for your permission to go to Makeni, but I would like you to be aware that I am going there tomorrow"*, knowing full well that the High Commissioner could not officially sanction such a trip.

The next morning Mark went to Roland's office and before he set off with the driver, all the staff came out, gathered around the vehicle and said prayers for their safe return. Mark was very touched by this, but rather disconcerted that they felt the need to do so. He soon found out why. The road to Makeni had, apparently, been excellent when Sierra Leone became independent in 1961, but it was obvious that nothing had been done to maintain it. The tarmac had disintegrated, grass and weeds were everywhere. On leaving Freetown, 70 miles of potholes made progress very slow, but luckily Abu, the driver, seemed to know every one of them.

On the way there were numerous road blocks and checkpoints, manned mainly by manic men in various types of uniform and young boys with sad staring eyes carrying weapons almost as big as themselves. It was never clear whether they were supporters of the Government or the rebels, but they all had one thing in common – they wanted money which they called a 'morale booster'. There were also other road blocks near villages where enterprising local people had dug holes in the road. They pretended to be repairing them – and they, too, wanted money! Seeing a white man in a truck with a Baptist school's name and logo on the side, they all presumed that Mark must be a minister and referred to him as 'Father'. Soon Mark ran out of small change so the only 'morale booster' he was able to give them was

Joseph Kargbo

a blessing which seemed to reassure and please them greatly. At one checkpoint he was asked for his identity card. He had, on purpose, left his passport back in Freetown and the only form of identity he could find was an old National Trust membership card. This impressed the soldier; presumably he thought that if Mark was trusted by the Nation he must be a good man! It was a relief to arrive in Makeni three hours later.

Mark met the Paramount Chief, a tall, impressive man, who showed him one of his houses – large and empty – situated on a quiet side street. The Paramount Chief said that if we wished, he would be happy to rent it to us for a small sum of money. The return journey to Freetown took a very long time. By the time we got back to the HANCi office in Freetown, it was dark. An anxious Roland was waiting for us and was greatly relieved when we arrived.

A few weeks later we went back to Sierra Leone together; this was Caroline's first visit. We were shown around the various camps by Joseph, who was Roland's cousin. Caroline was horrified. Until her eyes were adjusted to the darkness in the stiflingly hot, grim airless place she clung on to Mark. She longed to gather up all the tiny children she saw and take them out of this hellhole.

Joseph was the main person running HANCi, as Roland still had his full-time job with the Baptist schools. Joseph was a lovely, lively person. Together we identified 40 little children aged from about three to seven, who had no

Joseph with children and staff living in the Paramount Chief's house

known surviving relatives. Working with HANCi we rented the Paramount Chief's large, old house in Makeni, as we all considered it to be the safest place in the country at that time.

We asked HANCi to find a carpenter to make a small bed, table and chair for each child, giving them something of their own. On Christmas Eve in 1996 HANCi collected the 40 small children from the various camps and took them to their new home. We telephoned HANCi the next day to see how the move had gone and we asked if the children liked their new beds. The reply was, *"No, they all slept on the floor cuddled up together!"* It was a lesson for us not to impose our own ways of doing things on people with a totally different background; the children had always slept on the floor, with the warmth and comfort of other bodies around them. In some ways the house was ideal as it was on a quiet back street. The children could go in and out easily and they became part of the local community. People often gave them fruit and treats as they passed by.

Over the years many kind people have sent us Teddies for Tragedies for the children. These hand-knitted teddy bears were made to a particular

On the balcony of their new home

pattern by people who wanted to give something personal and special to children who have suffered as a result of a trauma or tragedy. About nine inches tall, they are in different colours and very soft and cuddly. On one of our visits to Sierra Leone we

One of the four new houses

took 60 teddies with us to give to the children in Makeni. When we arrived at the home we gave one to each child and they were all very excited and loved them – or so we thought. A few days later we went back to the home and could not see any of the teddies, so we asked the children where they were. They told us they had killed them and showed us various dismembered remains. We found this a very disturbing example of what we came to understand as projected play. This is the way in which children who have experienced abuse or other terrors act out their inner fears and anxieties using their toys or dolls. Although the children all seemed happy and smiling, we could not see into their minds. We could only imagine what they had been through to cause them to do this.

The needs of such children were enormous and it soon became clear that the house in Makeni really wasn't big enough for so many of them. Fortunately we were offered a large piece of land just outside the town with some mango trees growing on it. We thought this was a perfect place and so we bought the land and constructed four houses for 15 children in each. We agreed with HANCi that each of the four houses would have a 'mother figure'. This worked out well. The children settled down happily and went to the local school. There was also a house for the 'home father', Peter Brima, and his family, and another for our two volunteers. There was a separate building which housed the kitchen and a large dining room/play area. HANCi then decided that a big wall should be built round the site to stop unauthorised people entering. There was a gate to let vehicles in – and, of course, this needed a guard to open and close it. This meant that the children were cut off from the community and we soon realised that it was a big mistake on our part.

Another mistake concerned the lack of electricity in Makeni at the time. HANCi asked if we could fund the purchase of a generator. As no-one else had electricity we said "No" and they said, "No-one else is looking after 60 little children like us!" On our next visit the first thing we heard was the thump, thump, thump, of a big old, diesel generator. Now, the only place that had electricity in the town was the children's home, yet further alienating them from those who saw themselves as being less fortunate than the orphans.

We arranged for two volunteers at a time to go out from the UK to help the local staff and, in particular, to organise activities for the children. Everything went well for about a year until the rebels decided to capture Makeni. As they advanced towards the town we ordered our two volunteers, Peter and Dominic, to leave immediately. Dominic went to the local post office where there was a telephone and miraculously managed to call us in the office in East Clyffe. He said that he thought he was safe and wanted to stay. Mark shouted down the telephone, "No. Get out now. Get on the next relief helicopter. That is an order." Fortunately Dominic obeyed and managed to get on the last flight out, ending up in Conakry, in Guinea, but without his passport. Meanwhile Peter was having a break with a few friends in a house by the sea just outside Freetown. They suddenly saw a group of rebels coming along the beach so they ran up the hill behind the house and hid in the bush for two days. When they thought the 'coast was clear' (quite literally!) they made their escape along the beach to a hotel from which, they had heard, expatriates were being evacuated. Eventually they were put in a helicopter to Lungi Airport which was also being besieged at the time. To their astonishment a French aircraft flew in and kept its engines running as evacuees ran onto it and, within a few minutes, it took off. Peter and Dominic had very lucky escapes! As the rebels got closer to Makeni there was an urgent need to move the children. Peter Brima and his staff led the children on foot along jungle tracks for about 45 miles heading north until they reached a little village called Kaponki, near the town of Kamakwie. It was an extraordinary achievement as most of the children were very young – the youngest was just a year old and the oldest about seven. It took many days and nights to reach Kaponki through difficult terrain. Fear of being discovered meant that they mainly walked by night and slept in the daytime – it was much safer that way.

Kaponki was a quiet, remote little village, hidden away in the jungle in an area which turned out to be controlled by the rebels under the command of a woman calling herself Major Sarah. Although she was aware of the children's presence, she allowed them to live there for 21 months, unharmed, but money was desperately needed to buy food for them. Getting money to Kaponki was a difficult and extremely dangerous task. Roland and one of his team, Kelfa Kargbo, a young man who later became his deputy, undertook several perilous journeys from Freetown, via Guinea, in order to reach Kaponki with the money hidden in their underpants. It often entailed walking along small jungle paths to avoid both sides in the conflict. Getting to Kaponki and back again to Freetown was treacherous. It was an extremely brave thing to do, but showed how much they cared about the children.

On 10 February 1998 the rebels closed in on Freetown . There was fierce fighting and brutality on the streets. As they got closer to HANCi's office, which was near the harbour, the staff decided to escape by boat. Joseph was shot in the shoulder, but the others managed to get him into the long boat as well as the motorbike which Joseph insisted must go with them. We had bought the motorbike for the team so that they could visit the children in the rural areas. Joseph was very proud of the bike. The boat became hugely overloaded with over 250 people on board. When they were near the safety of the opposite shoreline, the boat hit a rock and overturned. Sadly 165 people were drowned, including poor Joseph. One of Roland's teenage sons was also on the boat. For many days Roland did not know what had happened to him as no communications existed. Luckily he was a strong swimmer. Several weeks later his son appeared back at home in Freetown without any warning. He had survived the disaster.

As the news coming out of Freetown got worse, we were very worried about Roland, his family and staff; we tried, repeatedly, to contact him. One day Mark decided to have another go and called his home telephone number. To his delight and surprise Roland answered in a very quiet voice. Mark asked him where he was and Roland replied, *"Under the bed."* He explained in a muted voice that there was fierce fighting going on outside, that he had seen lots of dead bodies and right now his house was full of family and friends. He added that so far, they were okay. Freetown, a teeming city of desperate people, had fallen to the rebels who were murdering, raping and destroying everything. Many of the peacekeeping forces took refuge in their barracks, leaving the population to the mercy of drugged and depraved gunmen. Thousands died, their bodies left lying in the streets and along the seashore. Eventually the rebels were driven back out of the city into the bush once more.

Joseph's tragic death created a huge problem as he had been the key person running HANCi since Roland still had a full-time job with the

Seeing Joseph's new motorbike for the first time

schools. How could they now continue to operate? We realised that Mark had to go there again to meet up with Roland and discuss this dilemma. However, the main airport at Lungi was closed as it was in rebel hands, so Mark was forced to fly via Conakry in Guinea.

From Conakry he managed to get on a very small plane which took him to a tiny airstrip in Hastings, on the mainland ten miles outside Freetown. It was there that he met up with Roland. After a few days of going around the area and assessing the situation, Mark managed to arrange a flight back to Conakry. As they waited for the plane to arrive, he said to Roland, *"You know, if HANCi is going to survive, there is only one person who can make this happen."* Roland replied, *"Yes, I know. I have been praying for guidance and I have decided to resign as the Head of the Baptist Schools and devote my life to helping the children."* This was such a relief and an enormously selfless act. Our work in Sierra Leone could now continue.

As the situation worsened, however, we all became anxious about the children's continuing safety in Kaponki, fearing that they might be used as human shields. This fear led the HANCi team to plan a very daring rescue operation, even more difficult than the flight from Makeni. Kelfa volunteered to lead the evacuation just two days after his wedding and went in to collect the children and the staff. Under cover of darkness the first party of 46 young children, led by Kelfa, left Kaponki and walked out along jungle tracks. They hid by day for fear of being seen by somebody on the ground or spotted by helicopters. Eventually they reached a river. Here they climbed into dug-out canoes, went down the river and finally out to sea. After many dangerous miles they reached their destination – Freetown harbour! It was a miraculous escape, worthy of a Hollywood film. The remaining children and staff followed a few days later. Our next task was to find somewhere for all the

Kelfa Kargbo

children to live. HANCi, with our help, succeeded in renting some big houses in Freetown.

It was from there, one day, that Roland telephoned us saying that Tenneh, one of the small girls in one of our homes, had a bullet in her head. She had not been well, complaining of headaches, and the doctor had taken her to the hospital for an X-ray. The image was extraordinary. It showed a bullet, probably from an AK47 rifle, near her eye. The hospital staff in Sierra Leone said that if the bullet moved she would most certainly die and therefore she needed an operation urgently. However, they could not do it in Sierra Leone. When Roland told us this, we asked him to send the X-rays by the quickest possible means and two days later they arrived. We were shocked and amazed by the clarity of the film and the fact that Tenneh was still alive.

We immediately contacted our friend James Ruddy at the *EDP* and, having told him the story, asked if he could help us. We sent him the X-rays and James took them to the Norfolk and Norwich Hospital. A maxillofacial surgeon, Mr Jeffrey Cheney, looked at the X-rays and said that he thought that he would be able to remove the bullet. The hospital kindly agreed to undertake the

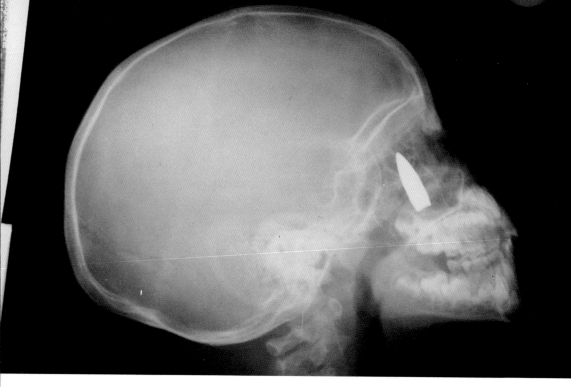

operation and cover all of the medical costs. Our next big challenge was to get Tenneh a visa and bring her back with us to the UK. The British High Commission in Freetown was very helpful and we booked flights and made all the necessary arrangements.

Realising that Tenneh's story would create a great deal of media interest when news of it got out, we agreed with James and the *EDP* that we would all keep it secret until Tenneh arrived in England as we didn't want a media scramble trying to get out to Sierra Leone to find her first. A few days later we flew out to Sierra Leone with James and we went up-country to collect Tenneh. There was no apparent sign of her condition, but we discovered she was profoundly deaf; we think this was a result of lassa fever. We had not met Tenneh before and we were absolutely amazed by the trust that she put in us right from the start. Looking back now, this seems extraordinary. Three white people she had never seen came to take her away and she did not put up any resistance.

Caroline took her hand and we got into the car. We drove to the ferry, went on the one-hour boat trip across the harbour and drove to the airport. She had only ever been in one vehicle before, and that was to the hospital, but she took it all in her stride. As Tenneh was deaf and we could not communicate with her easily, it was difficult for us to understand her emotions or apparent

Tenneh on the ferry

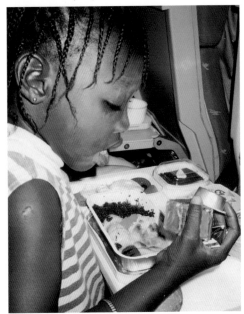

Tenneh inspecting her meal on the plane

lack of them. She was very calm and placid and we wondered what was going on in her mind as the journey continued. Tenneh watched the big, white aeroplane arrive, and without any fuss climbed aboard. She sat between us as we took off for our night flight to England. Food was eventually served with a choice of fish or meat. We thought Tenneh would probably like fish and we chose the meat for ourselves. How wrong we were! When she saw our food her hand came across and she started taking the meat off our plates. By now we were exhausted and just wanted her to go to sleep. The lights were dimmed and the film (no choice back then!) was shown. It was *Babe*, the story of the talking pig! What can Tenneh have thought? She had been taken by three white strangers, travelled on a boat for the first time, and was now up in the sky in a big white bird watching a film about a talking pig!

As we were flying back to England the *EDP* featured the story with the X-ray photos in that morning's edition. They had a world scoop and the global media reacted immediately.

On our arrival at London Heathrow early in the morning, we were surprised to see Immigration and Customs officials getting on to the plane. They looked around and asked if the little girl sitting with us was Tenneh Cole. They told us to remain seated while all the other passengers got off as there was a phalanx of journalists waiting for us. They checked our passports and we were cleared by Customs onboard the plane. As we entered the airport building we met a barrage of flash bulbs and television cameras. Michael Dewar, who was our PR consultant, had arranged a conference room for us at the airport and we were escorted to it surrounded by the paparazzi. We were given seats behind a long table on a stage and Tenneh sat on Caroline's knee, playing with a model plane she had been given by Sabena, the airline we used. She seemed totally unfazed by what was happening. Numerous questions were asked and more photos were taken. Following this, James took Tenneh by car to the Norfolk and Norwich Hospital. He left her in the wonderfully loving care of the nurses in the children's wing who made an enormous fuss of her. Jeffrey Cheney and his team carried out a detailed examination and could not find any sign as to how the bullet got into her skull. He thought it might have been

Our arrival at Heathrow

At the press conference with James Ruddy

a tumbling bullet which was falling out of the sky and had lost velocity and could possibly have gone through the soft, top part of her head. It was behind her right eye and dangerously close to her brain. He agreed that it had to be removed and he thought he could do it.

A few days later Jeffrey operated on Tenneh and we waited anxiously for news. Tenneh's story and pictures of the X-ray had 'gone global', so the pressure on Jeffrey that morning must have been enormous. It was a huge relief for all of us when we heard that the operation had been successful.

Eastern Daily Press

WEDNESDAY, MAY 15, 1996 — THE COUNTRY'S BEST-SELLING REGIONAL MORNING NEWSPAPER — 37p

SKILL: Norfolk consultant Geoffrey Cheney with the bullet he removed from Tenneh's head
Picture: SIMON FINLAY

OUT AT LAST ■ This is the bullet which was in orphan Tenneh's head for 16 months, causing a life-threatening infection

Tenneh's timebomb

We had made it absolutely clear to everyone, in articles and interviews, that we would take Tenneh back to Sierra Leone when the doctors considered her ready to go. We had obtained an emergency visa for her to come to the UK for the operation on the understanding that she would, after her recovery, return to her own country. But most importantly, taking everything into consideration, we felt strongly that it was in her long-term best interests to go back to Sierra Leone and the people she knew. We were amazed, however, by the consternation and outrage this caused amongst some who thought we were being heartless in sending her back to such a poor country in which atrocities against children were still being perpetrated. We received some extraordinary letters; one or two people even said that God had sent Tenneh to them and when and where could they collect her. During her convalescence the media interest continued and the *EDP* ran an appeal to fund her future; many people sent in generous donations which are now still being used to fund her training as a hairdresser, and a small home for her.

After two weeks James Ruddy took Tenneh back to Sierra Leone where there was great rejoicing on her arrival. She had become an icon for the suffering in her country. The other children were thrilled to see her and she was obviously very happy to see them and be back with the familiar faces that she knew.

We would like you to accept this book as a token of our appreciation of the wonderful support you have given us. We do hope that you will enjoy reading it.

With our great thanks and very best wishes,

Mark & Colluie.

Hope & Homes
for Children

Numb3rs

When children end up in orphanages, they are reduced to numbers and bad things happen to them.

Often they suffer such appalling abuse and neglect that they are unable to develop properly, some even die.

Hope and Homes for Children are global leaders in child protection reform. We work alongside governments, community groups and other charities to strengthen vulnerable families, close orphanages, and to ensure all children grow up with the love and protection of a family.

Between now and 12 December, every donation we receive will be doubled by the UK government. With your support the Hope and Homes for Children's Numb3rs appeal can end the need for orphanages and save lives.

Every child has the right to be more than a number. The time to act is now.

Visit www.notanumb3r.org

The only numbers you need to know.

1 Donation. **2** wice the Impact. For **3** Months.

Act Now

Tenneh holding hands with her great friend, Ami Jabati, as she and the other children welcome her back after her operation

In the aftermath of the conflict one of the most vulnerable groups of children were the young girls in the country who had been taken as sex slaves by the rebels and had produced children. When they were reunited with their families many were often not welcomed back. One girl said that this was even more distressing than having been taken by the rebels in the first place. We were extremely fortunate that Soroptimist International, the global organisation of professional and business women, chose to support our work with these young mothers in 2007 as their Quadrennial Appeal. Over four years they raised the amazing sum of more than £1 million thereby saving the lives of countless mothers and their babies, giving them a future together.

A group of young mothers

We built a training centre in the southern city of Bo specifically to give some of these girls training so that they had a skill and more chance of getting a job. They could choose to train in dress-making, hairdressing, cooking or tie-dyeing. Courses ran for a year, at the end of which they were given a

diploma and the necessary materials for their chosen work, such as a new sewing machine or saucepans, to get them started. A crèche was set up at the Centre to look after the girls' babies while they were training. It was extremely successful. We went out to Sierra Leone with Audrey Paisey for one of the graduation ceremonies. This was attended by the girls' families who were obviously very proud. It was really very moving and uplifting to see these girls leaving the Centre with such pride in their achievements and hope for their future.

We also had a training centre in Kissy on the outskirts of Freetown where girls learnt dress-making and hairdressing and the boys developed carpentry or engineering skills. One girl we met in Kissy was typical of so many others. She was about 17, had a six month old baby and lived in a one-room tin shack with her bedridden grandmother. The shack was on a slope and sewage, from the mass of humanity existing further up the hill, ran right by the entrance. The girl had to look after her granny who told us she just wanted to die. She felt she was an enormous burden for her granddaughter whose baby also needed constant care. They had absolutely no income at all. For the three of them to survive, this girl had no option other than to sell herself regularly. Such memories haunt us and Audrey still.

Peace for everyone in this tortured country came on 14 May 2001 when a treaty was signed. People started returning to their villages and we began the process of reintegrating children with their families. This entailed members of HANCi travelling round the country trying to locate and identify surviving members of the children's families and helping them to rebuild their lives so that they could become self-sufficient. To support this programme we started a farm just outside Makeni and named it The Vicky Hunter Farm Resource Centre after a great supporter in our Vale of York Support Group. Vicky very sadly died, leaving two young girls, soon after her family had hosted Roland and Kelfa during an HHC conference we held in York. Shortly before she died, she told Mark that having the two of them to stay had been very special for her and her family. At the Centre palm oil seedlings, kasava and all manner of local plants and vegetables were cultivated and pigs, goats, chickens and ducks were bred. All of these were distributed to needy families to help them become self-sustaining.

Since 1994, working together with HANCi, we have helped thousands of children and their families through extremely difficult times. HANCi became a well-respected, effective and experienced NGO, supported by many big organisations such as Comic Relief, DFID and UNICEF.

Saplings being grown in the Farm Resource Centre

Now that HHC is totally focussed on being the catalyst for the eradication of institutions for children and the Government of Sierra Leone is not in a position to commit to this, we decided in 2013 that the time was right for us to conclude our work in the country. Having been personally so involved in Sierra Leone and knowing so many of the children, we were sad to leave, although we knew in our hearts that it was the right decision for HHC.

However, we are very pleased that Tom Dannatt, the son of General Lord Dannatt, one of our Patrons, has founded his own charity in Sierra Leone called Street Child of Sierra Leone (SCoSL). He has taken over and expanded many of our programmes in partnership with the former HANCi team and is doing great work there.

Despite all their suffering and poverty and all they have been through, the people of Sierra Leone are the most cheerful and optimistic we have ever met.

ॐ

New Homes At Last
Mozambique

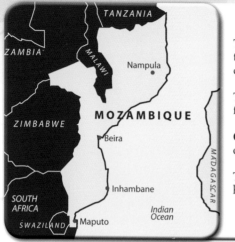

1996 - 1999

The Situation: In the 1980s a civil war caused the deaths of about one million people and drove five million from their homes.

The Problem: Countless children lost their families and their future.

Our Initial Plan: To build homes for 100 orphans in Beira.

The Outcome: We completed the homes and handed them over to a local NGO.

"Poverty is the worst form of violence."
Mahatma Gandhi

Soon after my arrival in Beira I went to visit the beautiful new homes that we have built for over one hundred orphaned children at the Manga Centre. As I walked around, a little hand tugged insistently on my shirt, and Zinho introduced himself impeccably, but then his English faultered. "Teatro da Crianca" ('Children's Theatre') he stated and pointed. I followed him to one of the new homes, where ten of his young friends were gathered in the corner of a tiny room. Immediately they launched themselves into a series of sketches – the confidence, the way they threw themselves into their characters, their sheer enjoyment and desire to entertain were a joy to behold. It was easy to forget that all of these children had lost their homes, families and had lived the very harshest of tender young lives. They were between eight and ten years old, but knew more about life and survival than we will ever know.
(James Whiting)

Mozambique was at peace at long last, but there was still unbelievable suffering and poverty. Bitter fighting had gone on for 25 years, ripping apart homes, families and lives. Many youngsters had fled into the bush, living in grass huts and surviving on roots and wild fruits. Others were forced to join roving militia as child soldiers, slaughtering innocent villagers without thought. Some had even been forced to kill their own mothers. Others had witnessed the killing of family members and had themselves been tortured. Many of the children who were left alive in 1992, at the end of the war, were living on the streets. They were bewildered, hungry and alone, with nowhere to live and no-one to care for them – and without hope.

In 1996 Bohdan Rymarenko, who had become our volunteer International Coordinator, heard about a Swiss lady who was working with homeless children in the port town of Beira. She had formed a small local NGO called ASEM (Association pour les Enfants de Mozambique) and created a safe centre for the children. Their living conditions were far from ideal and they needed proper homes to get them out of their emergency accommodation.

Following an initial visit by Bohdan, we went out to Mozambique for a week to see what we could do. Dozens of chattering children greeted us when we arrived at the Centre. Their small hands reached out to clutch our own in that magical greeting that we have now experienced so often in Africa.

We were amazed at their sense of joy, after so much hurt in their young lives. There was a great buzz of activity and excitement as they took us around and showed us the two large bamboo huts where they slept, the kitchen where great pots of rice and vegetables were bubbling away, and the all-purpose community room where they gathered together, ate their meals and where creative activities took place. Their classroom huts were nearby.

The Centre was on the outskirts of Beira. The bamboo buildings stood on a large area of flat, sandy ground and alongside them was that most vital necessity for small boys...a football pitch! This was 'home' for 130 children.

Over the next few days we spent time talking, playing and eating with the children and we were struck by their enthusiasm to learn, their energy and their constant laughter. It was difficult to match their positive spirit and joy for life with the horrific experiences they had suffered. We were told many heart-breaking stories which had led to each of them living in the Centre. But now, they were very much alive, alert and full of hope.

While we were there the sun shone fiercely, the ground was baked hard and the holes in the bamboo and grass huts provided much-needed ventilation. But life was very different when the torrential rains came. The area was turned into a quagmire. The buildings leaked and needed constant repair and patching up.

The local authority had given ASEM a large plot of land surrounded by trees in a rural area called Manga further out of town. This was the perfect spot to create a permanent centre with proper buildings and facilities and ASEM badly needed our financial support to do this. Having been so impressed by the organisation, the way it was run and, most importantly, by the children themselves, we agreed to help them and drew up plans to build seven houses.

The building work started in October 1997 with the children making some of the bricks. While this was going on, we sent out two volunteers at a time to help look after the children, teach them English and organise events and activities. Hannah and Rory, two of our enthusiastic, young volunteers, spent six months there and, amongst other things, taught them Scottish country dancing and cricket! Chess was also a craze and the children were very good at it, as James Whiting found out when he made his first HHC visit to Mozambique. After two other special volunteers, Edward and Alison left, they wrote, *'The evening we said goodbye, we left the children with*

our pockets full of sweets and peanuts that they had given us. This gesture will always remind us of the warmth and affection they all showed us. Having them as friends for six months, and seeing what a positive outlook they have and how receptive they are to anyone who takes the time to encourage them, made us both very happy.'

David Hodson with the Manga Centre football team

We became frustrated by the slow progress in the building programme and the numerous excuses given, such as illness, lack of materials and excessive rains. It was obvious that it was going to take much longer than we originally thought and we were concerned about the costs and possibility of corruption. We needed a permanent presence there, such as a project manager, to oversee the building programme and keep an eye on the expenditure. We wanted someone who was used to taking responsibility, was tough, resilient and tactful, able to deal with all the challenges of different personalities, and vested interests. Following a talk that Mark gave in a local church near Salisbury one Sunday morning, David Hodson introduced himself to us saying that he would

like to do anything he could to help us. After talking with him for some time, we realised that he was just the right person for the job; he had recently retired from being a Major in the Royal Marines!

Under very difficult circumstances David did a remarkable job and early in 1999 the first two new homes in the Manga Centre were opened, providing a real haven for 14 small children. He wrote at the time, *'Building work at Manga is proceeding at a reasonable pace despite the best efforts of the wet season to slow things down.*

The new Centre under construction

Although the Centre still very much looks like a building site, with the volunteers' house receiving its final coats of paint, and the next building, the crèche, growing daily, the gradual transformation of the project, from drawing into reality, is exciting to see. Water, electricity and telephones are due to be connected and operational very shortly and the accommodation for the volunteers will be ready by the end of March. We are looking forward to moving-in day!'

Soon afterwards Caroline, our volunteer out there at the time, sent us a letter saying, *'Work at the Centre is going very well. I have set up a new English programme for the staff and students and every day I have to add new pupils to the classes! I feel really settled here and I think I have finally won the battle to be accepted by the local staff.'*

The whole project was completed and the Centre was opened on 31 July 1999. We had hoped to continue working in partnership with ASEM and the children, but it had become clear that we were not needed once we had completed the building programme. We had achieved what we had set out to do – build a wonderful Centre – but ASEM did not want our help in running it. Having got to know the children, we were disappointed about this, but happy to have given them more hope for the future.

ॐ

THE LEGACY OF LUNACY
ALBANIA

1997 - 2007

The Situation: 40 years of a brutal Communist regime resulted in desperate poverty.

The Problem: Numerous babies were abandoned at birth and children existed in terrible orphanages.

Our Initial Plan: To provide a home for the 50 infants we found in a block of flats.

The Outcome: We completed this and eventually got all the children into family care.

"With this money I will build homes for the poor. It is in the home that love begins."
Mother Teresa on receiving the Nobel Peace Prize in 1979

We found 50 children, all under three years of age, most of them sitting silently in a long line on their potties, crammed into two small rooms on the second floor; they had nowhere to play. The place was smelly and stuffy. No windows were open. We were told that germs would fly in from outside. Amongst the children was one little boy called Mondi, who had Down's Syndrome. He was lying on the floor, under a cot which had its sides down to floor level, so forming a cage to keep him in. His situation and that of all the other toddlers and babies was desperate.

This awful scene confronted us on our first visit to Albania. The country was totally isolated from the world for 46 years, from 1944, by the brutal, and seemingly mad, Communist dictator, Enver Hoxha. The nearest equivalent regime today is North Korea. The Albanian borders were sealed by guards and no-one was allowed in or out of the country without a special permit. Any form of communication with the outside world was forbidden and the punishment for being caught was a long term of imprisonment leading, in many cases, to death. Children were indoctrinated at school, including being told it was their duty to report their parents if they heard them making derogatory remarks about Enver Hoxha or saw them breaking any of the numerous petty and controlling laws which were designed to completely subjugate the population and control their every thought, movement and action.

Our first visit was made after David Grubb, of FTC, visited us at home to discuss an idea that he thought might interest us. At that time FTC was taking food aid into Albania. He suggested that we should start a joint project in which HHC would build a home for abandoned children and FTC would supply all the necessary support for running it. Since this sounded like a possible idea for a new project, we flew out to Albania and met up with Colin Raine who was running the FTC project there.

Extreme poverty and suffering were still very evident when we made this first visit in 1997, seven years after Enver Hoxha was overthrown. We quickly became aware of the dire situation the country was in and for the first time we realised what 'freedom of speech' really meant.

After spending a few days visiting various children's establishments we were totally shocked by the poverty and the terrible conditions in which the children were living. Then we heard about some babies and very young children who were being kept in an apartment block above some shops in the port town of Durres and, on the last day, we were taken to see them.

The apartment building

We were saddened and horrified by what we found. 30 tiny children were existing in squalor. Immediately we knew we had to do something to get them out of this dreadful place. We were told that they used to be in a far better building, but it had been taken over by the local authorities for another purpose. As a result the children had been moved to this totally unsuitable second floor, two-room apartment where they could never go outside. We just had to find somewhere better for them to live, but it soon became obvious that this was going to be a real problem. It proved to be even more difficult than we had at first anticipated.

A few months later, FTC decided to pull out of Albania saying that it was too difficult, dangerous and corrupt to continue working there. David Grubb advised us to do the same. By now, however, we had been to the country several times and knew the children. On one of our visits a features writer from *Harpers & Queen* joined us and published a moving account of the plight of the children. There was no way we could abandon them to their fate, so we decided to carry on with our plan even though FTC was leaving the country. Since we had to return to England we asked Colin Raine to work on our behalf and try to find a new place for the children.

The local authority suggested a big, disused, Government office building on the outskirts of Durres. Colin went to look at it. What he was not told before he went was that there were several hundred squatters living there. They became very angry when he told them why he had come and they chased him out of the building. So that was that.

On 31 August 1997, Princess Diana was killed in Paris, a tragedy no-one will ever forget. Thousands of bouquets of flowers, toys and teddy bears were left outside Kensington Palace on the grass as an expression of sympathy and loss. Some weeks later, just before Christmas, it was decided that they had to be moved, but clearly it was not appropriate to throw everything away. Rotary International in Great Britain and Ireland (RIBI), who had made a commitment to support our project

in Albania, contacted us to say that they had been given hundreds of these teddy bears. They asked if we would like to take some of them out for the children in Albania. We agreed and about 100 bears of different shapes and sizes were delivered to us. Realising this could be a good news story, Caroline contacted her cousin, Virginia Ironside, the journalist, and suggested she might like to come with us to give the bears to the children and, possibly, write a story too. She immediately agreed and suggested that Will, her son, who had just qualified as a film cameraman, should also come. Will jumped at the chance and contacted a member of the *BBC News* team who expressed an interest in showing the footage on our return.

A few days later, just before Christmas, the four of us flew out. Virginia and Will were horrified by the state of the little children, and Will took some excellent film of us giving them the teddies. Arriving back at Heathrow Airport a BBC dispatch rider met us and rushed the film to the studios where it was edited and shown on various news bulletins that same evening. Virginia also wrote a moving article which appeared on the front page of *The Independent*.

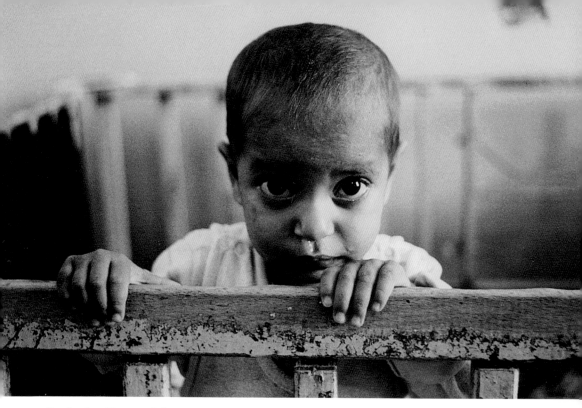

Both the film and the article were very powerful and caused a great response. The whole idea of Diana's tribute teddies being given to abandoned babies in a loveless orphanage in Albania touched the hearts of many people who contacted us and started supporting our work. One of these was a young mother who had recently had her first baby. As she wrapped up little Christmas presents for her, she saw us on the BBC news. She called us the next day saying that she was so distressed she could not sleep that night. Her name was Claire Wright; she and her husband, Michael, who founded Riviera Travel, have been the most amazing supporters ever since. Later, Claire opened and ran our Northern Support Group office in Burton-on-Trent, as a volunteer, for many years and she has also visited several of our projects.

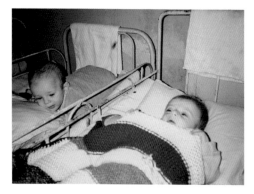

Back in Albania Colin Raine was still trying to find suitable accommodation to make a home for the children. He called us one day to say that after many false starts, the local authority suggested another building – an old, disused school in Durres which needed a lot of work doing to it.

This was very exciting news at last and Mark said he would fly out to see it. A meeting with the Mayor of Durres was arranged for 15 February 1998 at 12 o'clock.

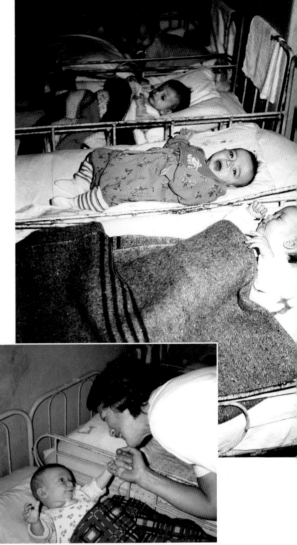

Mark and Colin arrived on time to be told that the Mayor was not in and they did not know when he would be back. We explained that Mark had flown out from England especially to see the Mayor and that we would wait until his return. Eventually the Deputy Mayor appeared and said that we might have a very long wait, perhaps until Monday! We asked him if he had seen the children and the conditions in which they were existing and he admitted that he had not. As the 'orphanage' was only five minutes' walk away, we suggested that they should go there immediately and 'propelled' the Deputy Mayor down the road and up the dirty stairs to the rooms in which the children were being kept. It was very warm, stuffy and disgustingly smelly. The Deputy Mayor, a large man, was wearing a big, warm coat; we took great delight at his discomfort. We asked him if he had children of his own and he said he had. Then we asked him if he would be happy if his children had to live in such conditions. He replied, *"No."* Looking very hot and uncomfortable, he could not get out of the room fast enough!

We walked back to the Mayor's office on the third floor of the building and continued to wait. An hour or so later we saw a big, black limousine draw up outside and a smart man, obviously the Mayor, got out and entered the building. After some time we were told that the Mayor had had to leave on very important business. We pointed out that his car was still outside and were told that the Mayor had already left the building, to which Mark replied, *"Mayors do not walk!"* After more waiting, we were shown into the Mayor's office. He was very friendly and apologised for any misunderstanding. We explained that we wanted to convert and repair the old school to make it into a lovely home for the children. Eventually the Mayor agreed with our plan and we shook hands. Mark told the Mayor that it was his birthday and the agreement was the best possible present he could ever have.

The building was in a terrible state; it had been vandalised and used as a public lavatory. The first thing that Colin did was to have a tall security fence put round it and he hired an armed guard to protect it. At first we were surprised by this but we were constantly being told by many people in the country, including Albanians themselves, that *"This is Albania!"* and we should not be surprised by anything.

This project was the first one that Rotary supported, so Mark made contact with the one and only Rotary Club in Albania. He was invited to attend their next committee meeting which turned out to be a finance meeting in Albanian. As Mark did not understand the language or finance, he found it rather tedious! However, at the end he explained our plans to rescue the babies and young children from the awful apartment in Durres and create a warm, loving home for them. After the meeting the Club Treasurer had a quiet word with Mark and explained that Albania was full of crooks and criminals and we would be 'ripped off' unless all the Rotary money was channelled through himself and the Club. Mark explained that this was not permitted under Rotary rules, but the man was insistent, showing him the Rotary badge in his lapel and saying, *"You have to trust me because I'm a Rotarian."* We later found out that he was an illegal arms dealer and one of the biggest criminals in the country. When the Club realised that they were not going to get their hands on any of our money they made no attempt to contact us further.

When we visited the country we often stayed at a very small hotel near the school building. One evening Mark was having dinner there on his own when the waiter, a teenage boy, started talking to him in broken English. He said he loved cars and showed Mark a photo of himself with a Mercedes which he said was his own. Mark asked him how old he was and what was the minimum age for a driving licence, to which the boy replied that he was 16 and the minimum age for a licence was 18, but he already had one! He explained that in Albania you could get anything if you had money. He then showed Mark a photograph of himself at school, carrying his own Kalashnikov rifle! He explained that he got his money by selling drugs. When Mark expressed his surprise and disapproval of this, the boy was very indignant saying that he only sold the drugs but would never use them himself!

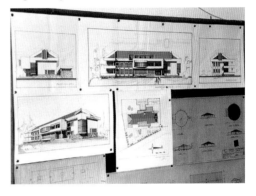

An Albanian lady architect drew up a very imaginative plan to modernise the old school building. It included replacing one long wall with large, sliding glass doors so that the children could go straight out on to the grass, and inside she created big, airy rooms. The whole building was totally transformed, although the standard of workmanship was of poor quality – very soon leaks occurred. As the work was going on, some of the staff started complaining that they did not want to move to the new building as it was away from the centre of the town. To overcome this problem we bought a minibus so that the staff could be shuttled back and forth for each shift. We had our suspicions that the minibus might have been stolen or illegally imported, but we had to trust those who signed the documents on our behalf.

The opening of the new home was duly arranged and a party of Rotarians who had been raising money for the new home, including Rodney Huggins, the RIBI President, booked their flights. Inevitably there were delays – the home was not completely finished nor were the children living in it, but the opening had to go ahead as planned. Mrs Sali Berisha, the President of Albania's wife, came to open the home. Because she was there, many other officials and the media came too, including the Deputy Mayor who had the gall to say to Mark, *"I told you we could do it if we worked together."* He had done

The new home

nothing at all. Mrs Berisha and the President had become good supporters of the project and helped Colin by 'oiling wheels' when necessary, which was quite often. She had been a teacher, spoke good English and impressed us with her genuine compassion and sincerity, qualities which seemed to be rare in the country.

Colin and his two key men, Adi and Turi, faced enormous difficulties during the building phase, including physical threats from people who did not support the project and corruption by others who wanted to benefit from it. At one stage there was a violent insurrection in the country, following the collapse of a Pyramid Investment Scheme and Colin, along with other expatriates, had to be evacuated from the beach outside Durres by Italian marines in a landing craft. In the confusion the marines opened fire on those they were trying to evacuate and a man next to Colin was shot and wounded. Colin was one of the first expatriates to return two weeks later, after order (or what passes for that in Albania) had been restored.

The builder and architect with Colin Raine (right)

It was not possible to get good quality children's furniture in Albania so Colin and his wife, Barbara, went to a factory in Bulgaria and ordered suitable furniture to be made to specific measurements. Shortly before the children moved in, Caroline went out taking with her a great number of beautifully handmade quilts from some of our wonderful supporters who had made them specifically for the new cots in the home. Val, our first volunteer in Albania, went with her to make beds, hang curtains and put up pictures and decorations. Val wrote afterwards, *'Not only have the lives of the children been improved beyond recognition but so too has the morale and esteem of the staff.'* On our next visit we took them all out one evening – apart from those on duty – to a local pizzeria to celebrate. Most of them were women and many told us that they had never been taken out to a restaurant before.

We went out to visit the children on several occasions; it was lovely to see how much happier they were in their new environment. However, it was obvious that it was not going to be so quick or easy to get the Director and staff to change their attitudes and behaviour, which had been ingrained in their brains since birth. We learned that it is easier to create a beautiful home for children than to change the mentality and working practices of the staff. In modern 'computer speak' they needed 'rebooting'. They required training and constant supervision. Since it was going to be almost impossible to find an Albanian person capable of doing this, we advertised for volunteers to go there to help with the process. Over the next few years many volunteers contacted us and came to our East

Children in their new home

Three of our volunteers

Ursula, one of our volunteers, on her 21st birthday

Clyffe office to be interviewed and briefed. We will always remember them and the truly remarkable work they did to help both the staff and children.

One person whose CV suggested that she had the right skills and character to be a volunteer was a young woman called Jacqui Cole. She came to the

office for an interview and we both thought that she was great, full of energy and enthusiasm. She started in the spring of 2000 as a volunteer and after a few months we made her our Training Manager. Shortly after, we appointed her as our Country Director. Jacqui stayed there for three and a half years, working in possibly the most difficult environment of all the countries in which we were operating.

The children in the home were constantly ill because of the total ignorance of basic hygiene practices of the local staff. Baby milk bottles were passed around from one child to another and never properly cleaned or sterilised. Jacqui obtained bottles of sterilising solution and taught the staff how to wash and sterilise the bottles hygienically. A few days later

Jacqui with some of the children

she saw one of the staff take a bottle out of the solution and rinse it under the tap. Tap water in Albania was definitely not something anyone should drink – you never knew what might come out of the pipe! The woman told Jacqui that the resident doctor herself had told them that they had to do this.

There was a large store room in the home run and fiercely guarded by a large woman in a white coat who had the only set of keys. When she eventually let us look inside it one day we were horrified and bewildered to see it piled high with items that were badly needed, but her regulations said that stores were for storing. She was accountable to the Ministry who could and did make snap inspections to make sure that all items were there. If they were not, she would lose her job. Problems like these faced Jacqui every day, but without hesitation she told everyone and anybody, including Ministers, what was right and what was wrong. There were no grey areas with Jacqui – it was either black or white.

One of the great battles she fought for most of the time she was in Albania was the case of three Roma siblings whose parents had been imprisoned for trying to sell them. Such was their desperate poverty that they had already sold five of their children, the last one for the equivalent of £25 and a black and white television set. The three in the home, two boys and a girl, were beautiful children. We were all most concerned about them as they had very little chance of a happy long-term future and none at all of being adopted together in Albania. There really was only one hope for them – that someone from another country would rescue them. Miraculously this is what happened. International adoption, in very exceptional cases such as this one, offers a solution. A very caring and loving couple came to the home, quickly bonded with the three children and wanted to adopt them. But there was a problem …

The children's birth parents had had their parental rights for the two oldest children taken away from them by the Albanian courts; this meant that they could be adopted but not the youngest child who had been born in prison. The potential parents were adamant, as were we, that they wanted to keep the siblings together. Jacqui applied to the court to have the parents' parental rights removed for the youngest child. However, the Ministry of Justice delayed, procrastinated and kept putting off hearing the case. Eventually after two years Jacqui managed to bring the matter to the attention of the Court of Human Rights in Strasbourg, and it was actually raised at an international conference attended by the Albanian Minister of Justice who was openly rebuked for not dealing with the case earlier. Shortly afterwards the case was heard and the decision made to remove the parental rights for the third child. After the court hearing Jacqui met the Justice Minister who said to her, *"Jacqui Cole, you are a very powerful woman."* Power was something they understood, feared and respected. Very soon these three children left the home for their new life abroad. Jacqui has been to see them several times and still hears from them occasionally. All is well with the family and, as in many fairy stories, we hope *'they will live happily ever after'*.

It was very important that the older children in the home should go to a kindergarten and mix with the other children in the very impoverished community that surrounded the home. It just so happened that there was a derelict old school building outside the back gate and we managed to secure funding to rebuild and equip it as the much needed kindergarten. This became a great asset to the whole community and the appointed Head Teacher was an exceptional person. She loved all children and would come and help those in the home in her spare time.

Jacqui was asked to help the Government transform their childcare services. The country had an enormous number of problems to deal with including trafficking of children abroad for spare body parts. It was an uphill and exhausting struggle for her since any form of work ethic was totally unheard of in Albania. Apparently Enver Hoxha had declared that people employed by the Government should not smoke while they were working. The result was that everyone smoked all the time instead of working! Although Jacqui loved what she was doing, she decided in the spring of 2003 that it was time to return to England.

Audrey Paisey at the opening of one of the homes

We advertised for a replacement and, amongst others, a woman from the USA applied; she seemed to have just the right experience for the job. We could not afford to fly her to the UK, so we interviewed her by telephone (before the days of Skype!). We also asked her to send a video tape telling us about herself. Based on this information we employed her. It was a big mistake. She undid much of the good work and progress made by Jacqui. Georgette Mulheir, who was our European Manager based in East Clyffe at the time, flew out and asked the woman to leave. Fortunately Kerry Hall, who had been doing stirling work in Romania, agreed to take the Albanian programme on to the next stage.

Despite the much improved conditions we had provided for them, it was obvious that the children craved love and more individual attention.

Whenever anyone went there they always ran to greet them with their arms up in the air, wanting to be hugged and cuddled. This was not a natural thing for a child to do with complete strangers and we were determined to reintegrate the children within the Albanian community, and if possible with their own biological families.

Over the course of the next year Kerry succeeded in finding families for many of the children, but for 17 of them, for various reasons, this was not possible. In order to get these out of the orphanage and into a more natural type of family environment, we bought two ordinary houses (one for eight children, the other for nine) in Durres which we adapted and equipped and the children moved into them. Caroline went out with Jacqui and Audrey for the official opening of the homes on 14 March 2006. The children had already settled in and were beginning to enjoy their new life. It was a very happy day and a successful conclusion to our project in Albania. We handed over everything we had created to the local authorities in the hope, rather than the expectation, that the homes would continue to be run to a high standard.

෧

The children in their new Shkozet family group home

CAROLINE'S DREAM
ROMANIA

SLOVAKIA
UKRAINE
HUNGARY
Baia Mare Sighet
MOLDOVA
Cluj
Bacau
Timisoara
Sibiu
Brasov
ROMANIA
• BUCHAREST
SERBIA
BULGARIA
Black Sea

1997 -

The Situation: 24 years of a terrible Stalinist regime under Ceauşescu, resulting in desperate poverty, ended in 1989.

The Problem: Over 100,000 children existed in shocking State institutions.

Our Initial Plan: To rescue 60 babies whom we found abandoned on the top floor of a hospital.

The Outcome: We rescued all the babies and are now helping to reform the country's childcare system including the closure of all the institutions for children.

"Children in institutions go through hell on earth. Hell is a place without love."
Stefan Darabus

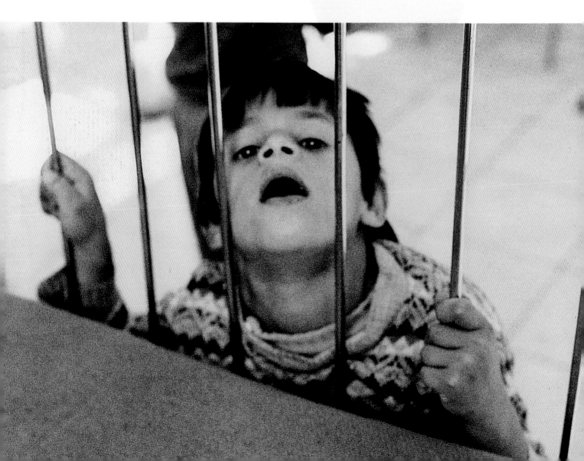

We were totally unprepared for what happened next. The Director opened a door and we were hit by the stench of urine and faeces. Inside 15 babies lying in cots were covered in their own excrement. No sound came from them … There was complete silence. At the far end of the room were two women in white coats, smoking cigarettes and looking out of the window. We pointed out to the Director, in case he hadn't noticed, that the children were dirty. We asked why the women couldn't wash them and he explained that it was not their job as they were 'educators'. He added that it was difficult to produce clean clothes without functioning washing machines. There were three more rooms with 15 children in each, all in the same state. Before leaving the hospital the Director took us down to the cellar to show us the broken machines and staff washing the soiled nappies by hand. Across the room stained pieces of cloth were hanging from strings. These were the 'clean' nappies. Again the stench was overpowering.

Few of us will forget the horrific pictures we saw when the horror of the orphanages in Romania was exposed following the dramatic overthrow of Ceaușescu in 1992. Many people were so moved by the plight of the children that they acted in any way they could to alleviate their suffering. Lorry-loads of aid were taken out from the UK and other European countries, and builders and plumbers went to repair crumbling buildings. The response was amazing. We were asked on numerous occasions why we had not joined in the rush to help. We explained that so much was being done by so many people that we felt there was no need for us. What more could we do that others had not already undertaken? Eventually we were persuaded to go and have a look at the situation, so James Whiting went out with the Chief Executive of the Romanian Orphanage Trust. On his return we discussed possible options and then we went out to see the situation for ourselves in the hope that we would come up with a plan of action.

We flew to Bucharest and caught the night sleeper up to Baia Mare in the north of the country. Arriving at about 6.30am on a very cold, icy morning in 1997 we were met by a young Romanian, named Stefan Darabus, who spoke perfect English. At the time he was helping the Romanian Orphanage Trust as an interpreter. They generously lent him to us for the duration of our visit. Having checked into a soulless, Soviet-style hotel, we were taken by Stefan in his father's very old car to a hospital in a drab mining town called Cavnic, about an hour's journey from Baia Mare. Stefan had heard that there were some abandoned babies hidden away in the hospital and he thought that this would be a good place for us to start. How right he was. This was where we discovered the unwashed children and the broken washing machines.

On arrival we climbed the stairs to the Director's office. He was a smartly-dressed young man in his late 30s. He told us he was a paediatric specialist. He explained that they were looking after 60 children under the age of three. We asked him if he had any problems with which we might be able to help. He told us that because the washing machines were broken, nappies had to be washed by hand in cold water. He asked if we could buy him some new machines. In his smart office there were lots of fluffy toys high up on shelves around the walls. As we drank coffee he asked his assistant to bring in one of the children. A little girl in a pretty dress, aged about three, came in and performed a sort of song-and-dance act for us. As a reward the Director took down one of the fluffy toys for her to play with for a few minutes.

Following this we asked if we could see the other children. *"Of course"*, said the Director and led us down a corridor. Caroline asked if she could take photographs. Again he said, *"Of course."*

We returned to the car in a state of shock. The sights and smells that we had just experienced were overwhelming, but worst of all was the unnatural silence of the babies ... Theirs was *"A Silent Cry"* for love. They had already learnt at their tender age that even if they cried ... no-one came. Then and there we agreed that we had to get all the children out of that awful place as soon as possible. As Stefan drove us straight back to Baia Mare we discussed various options and agreed that we should buy six houses for the 60 children immediately. On our arrival back at the hotel we contacted a local businessman whose details we had been given. He happened to be a Rotarian and we asked him for his help. On our behalf he went round estate agents and got details of potential properties in Baia Mare and Sighet, another town about an hour away. We spent the rest of the week looking round many properties and working out what would have to be done to each to make them suitable for ten children, with staff funded by the local authorities.

A meeting with the Secretary General of Maramureş County was arranged for us. In his grand office in the large town hall we told him of our plan and, surprisingly, he agreed to it and asked very few questions. Looking back, we are amazed that he accepted our offer so easily as we had no experience of doing anything like this. We really had no idea how we were going to move the children out of the hospital and then look after them. The only certainty in our minds was that we had to do it – and as quickly as possible.

We found six houses which we thought would be suitable, four in Baia Mare and two in Sighet. One of our prerequisites was that they should be near to schools which the children could attend when they were old enough. We also chose ordinary houses in the community so that the children would be in as normal an environment as possible. After the usual endless negotiations and haggling over price, we arranged to buy the six houses.

The first house we bought in Sighet

Before we left, we went back to tell the Secretary General of our progress. He was very happy and gave us two 2-litre coke bottles full of his own homemade ţuică. An extremely strong and powerful Romanian spirit, it is made from apples; it is no wonder that he was happy. Back at the hotel we put a little of the ţuică into an ashtray and lit it – it practically exploded. On our departure from the hotel, we hid the two bottles behind pillars in the foyer and hoped someone else might enjoy them ... and be happy too!

It was obvious that we needed someone who had a lot more time and experience than we had to go out to Romania to organise and run this complicated and extremely sensitive project. Luckily we found Eric Lee who had worked in local authority social services in the north east of England; he had 30 years' experience including moving children out of institutions. He had also recently been to Romania to give a lecture to some of their social workers. Eric went out on a brief recce just before Christmas 1998 and two weeks later

Eric Lee

Stefan Darabus

Princess Marina at the opening ceremony

returned to Romania to begin the transfer process. At the time we were unaware of the significance of what we were embarking on. This was our first big deinstitutionalisation (DI) project.

Stefan had impressed us very much during our visit; he was undoubtedly a truly exceptional young man. We were dismayed when he told us that he had made a commitment to join the police force. We told him that if he ever had a change of heart, we would welcome him as one of our HHC staff in his country. A few days later he telephoned us saying that he wanted to take up our offer. He said his heart was with the children – and it has been ever since. Shortly afterwards he began working for us and for the last ten years, since 2004, he has been our Country Director in Romania.

We flew out for the opening of one of our first small homes, which was a very special occasion. It was attended by local dignitaries. Having heard about our work, a lady called Princess Marina Sturdza flew up to Baia Mare from Bucharest for the opening ceremony. Princess Marina is a descendent of several Romanian royal families. She was forced to flee the country during the communist regime and had been brought up mainly in Switzerland and Canada. Following the overthrow of Ceauşescu, Princess Marina returned to Romania, helping in many different ways to rebuild civil society in her country. After the opening we asked Princess Marina if she would consider becoming a Patron. She accepted immediately and has been a tireless advocate and supporter of our work ever since, visiting several of our country programmes including Sierra Leone. It was on this occasion, too, that we first met a young medical doctor, Dr. Delia Pop, who was Director of Alternative Residential Services for the local authority. Eric Lee later recruited Delia to work for HHC in Romania. Since 2003 she has worked at East

Dr. Delia Pop listening to a child's story

Boy and Bear amongst the 27 'I Spy' quilts made by Mary Shaw and her team

Clyffe and has been our Director of Programmes since 2007. Delia has become one of the most highly regarded exponents of DI in the world. The opening of that first home proved to be a good day for HHC!

After 16 months, having got all the children out of that awful institution and happily settled in their new small homes, Eric Lee decided to leave. In the spring of 2000 he was replaced as Country Director by Georgette Mulheir, a British graduate and experienced social worker, she had previously worked with the Romanian Orphanage Trust. She told us she spoke fluent Romanian. We asked Stefan to verify this after they met for the first time and, in a serious voice, he reported back to us, *"She does not speak fluent Romanian, she speaks impeccable Romanian!"*

Georgette in one of the homes

We went out to see Georgette after she had been there for some time. She told us that the team wanted to close three more institutions – a baby institution for about 100 children aged three and under; the notorious Camin Spital, which means 'special hospital' for children with disabilities (both in the

Inside Girdan

88

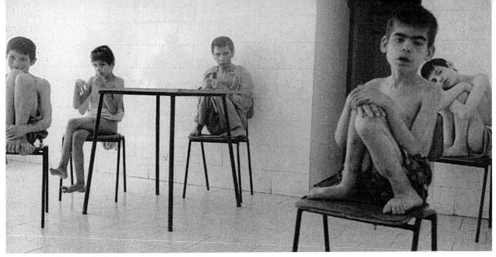

Inside the Camin Spital

town of Sighet) and thirdly, the Girdan Institution with over 100 boys and girls aged 7–17 years all crammed into a huge old house. Georgette took us to see all three of them; they were totally awful in different ways. It was obvious that there was terrible abuse of the children in Girdan, with young boys and girls and teenagers all mixed up together with very little supervision. At night there were only two members of staff on duty. Very often they were drunk. The water supply was intermittent and the toilets rarely worked. The children had no more than very basic education and no other organised activities. They just wandered around aimlessly.

The entrance to the Camin Spital

The tiny children in the baby institution in Sighet were all dressed in grubby white vests and pants with numbers stencilled on them. They 'existed' in rusty old cots crammed into small rooms. We watched a cleaner, in her dirty white coat, go around dusting with a brightly coloured rag. She put it down on a table near a cot for a moment and we saw a little hand come out between the bars. The child pulled the rag in and looked at it in wonder. Shortly afterwards the cleaner snatched it away and the child was back in her drab grey world.

Words cannot describe the horror that we found in the Camin Spital. 250 children with varying degrees of disability existed in six rooms on three floors. We were utterly overpowered and nauseated by the smell, the noise and the sight of the children. Many visitors found it too much to cope with and had to rush outside to be physically sick. The resident psychiatric doctor in the Camin Spital was a small, white-haired man in a white coat, who had worked there for over 30 years. On our first visit he took us round and told us about the children. Stopping at a cot in which a mature boy existed, he lifted up the boy's arm and let it flop down on the bed. *"Imbecile"*, he said. For him, all the children were imbeciles and incurables; he clearly had no compassion or empathy for any of them.

Somewhat daunted, we could not see how it would be possible to move all the children out of these three terrible places. With no experience of children who had special needs, which they all had, how would we cope? But Georgette, Delia and Stefan convinced us that we had to do it. We did not realise at the time just how capable and knowledgeable the three of them were. They also argued that if we could get all the children out of the Camin Spital, one of the most notorious institutions in Romania, we could close any of the others.

A few weeks later we went back to the Camin Spital with a camera crew who were making a promotional film for us about our work. To our amazement we had received permission from the local authority to do this. As always on arrival we went first to meet the Director in her office. She was very angry, having been told that HHC was going to close the institution, she saw herself losing her job. This was a typical reaction we were to discover – and one that should not have surprised us. For the majority of people working in institutions, it was their livelihood and they would probably find it very difficult to get other work. Understandably, perhaps, they put their own lives and the need to support their own families before considering what was best for the children. As we talked to the Director, or rather listened to her tirade, we were convinced that the telephone would ring at any moment cancelling our permission to film.

You can imagine how very anxious we were to get started. Then there was a knock on the door and a tall man and a woman came in. They introduced themselves saying they were from Norway and had previously visited the Camin Spital in the winter when the rooms were freezing. As a result, they had raised almost £60,000 to double-glaze all the windows. They asked what we were doing. It gave us enormous pleasure to tell them not to waste their money as we were going to close the place down and in a year's time there would be no children left in it. They were shocked and said it was impossible. We told them that not only was it possible, but it had to be done. Some time later, amazingly, they sent us the money they had raised.

Mark, Georgette and Edward opening presents on Christmas morning in the cold monastery

Some of the film which was taken that day featured in a very powerful video (later a DVD) which we called *A Cry For Love*. It helped to raise a lot of money towards our goal of freeing all the children from those three dreadful institutions.

Edward and children enjoying Christmas

In 2000 we thought it would be a great experience to go out to Romania for Christmas and spend some time with the families and children. Edward, our elder son, came with us. On Christmas Eve we drove up from Baia Mare to Sighet with Georgette, and stayed in an extraordinarily beautiful wooden monastery in a small village called Birsana. The Mother Superior was an

exceptionally dynamic and energetic woman who had galvanised support for the monastery which she built on the site of a previous one burnt down during Ceauşescu's time.

That evening we went carol singing around the village and were taken by the Mother Superior to have dinner with the family of the main building contractor. Georgette drove us there very slowly as the roads were icy. The Mother Superior, who was sitting in the front, got rather impatient and after a time said in Romanian the equivalent of *"Don't be a wimp - put your foot down!"* She was quite a character.

Early the next morning the church bells started clanging and Mark climbed up the winding wooden stairs to the belfry. There he found five nuns pulling five of the bell ropes, with one rope spare. One of the nuns passed it to him and indicated that he had to pull it. Fortunately there was no real peal, as we know it; the aim was clearly just to wake up everyone and say, *"Happy Christmas!"*

Later we joined the Mother Superior and some of the nuns for breakfast. A feast of ham, various cheeses and homemade bread was laid out. After grace we helped ourselves and started eating. We looked across the table and noticed that Edward was having a problem and was going bright red. Thinking that it was a piece of cream cheese he had put in his mouth, he discovered it was a large lump of pig fat. Poor Edward! Eventually he managed to 'dispose' of it in his napkin when no-one was looking.

The Mother Superior was very keen to acquire an unfinished house which was for sale just below the monastery. She said she wanted it so that she could provide a home for vulnerable girls. She took us to see it, but the house was locked up. Spying an open upstairs window and a builder's ladder nearby, she decided we should gain access that way. She sent Caroline up the ladder first and then quickly followed behind her. Unfortunately she got a bit too close

and Caroline accidentally kicked her in the face. To our surprise she found this hilarious. We thought the house would be ideal for a small home and the location seemed perfect with the monastery close by. The Mother Superior said she would keep an eye on it to make sure it was run properly. Feeling comfortable about this arrangement, we decided there and then to buy it.

Shortly after our return we had an 'Away Day' with a few key members of our team in East Clyffe; we wanted to discuss our thoughts and ideas. At one stage we decided that each of us should write down our dreams for the future of the charity which we would read out to the others. Caroline surprised all of us when she read hers; she said, *"My dream is that we close all the orphanages in Romania."* Our response was one of amused incredulity that she should even think that such a thing was possible. She explained that the images she had of children behind bars in their cots in institutions were, for her, the most shocking and upsetting sight of everything we had witnessed. Caroline said, *"They have no love, no freedom, absolutely nothing."*

At the time there were estimated to be over 100,000 children in about 650 State institutions – and we had managed to get just 60 children out of one of them. What a dream! As we all know, dreams rarely come true. It did not take long, however, before we all started talking about *'Caroline's Dream'* within the organisation, and the news of it spread outside to our supporters. It caught on. The dream turned into a goal and it gave us all a real motivating power. Over the next few years, as the momentum of our work in Romania increased, a target date of 2020 was set for the dream to become a reality.

On 21 May 1999 a personal tragedy occurred. Anna, the 17 year old daughter of our great friends, Bill and Kay Dawson, died very suddenly in Winchester Hospital just three hours after being admitted. Kay was our HHC receptionist at East Clyffe at the time and the loss of her daughter affected all of us deeply. We had known Anna since she was a baby and she had a special place in our

With Bill and Kay

Anna, the house mother, and the priest holding a plaque about Anna Dawson

hearts. She was at Sparsholt College in Hampshire at the time and she had a great love for all creatures … including her goldfish Gin and Tonic. Mark spoke at her funeral and said it was the most difficult talk he had ever given. The small village church at Sparsholt was so full that all her many young friends from the college had to sit on the floor around her coffin.

We wanted to remember Anna in a very special way and decided to raise funds for a home in Romania. In 2001 we went out for the opening of the home with Bill and Kay and other great friends, Jonathan and Gilly Edwardes, and Alison Jefferies, who all knew Anna. (Jonathan was Chair of our London Support Group and Alison of our Bath Support Group.) The home itself was a large farm house in a very pretty rural area on land owned by an elderly couple who had built a smaller house for themselves nearby. They still kept a few cows, sheep, pigs, chickens, dogs and cats, all of which Anna would have loved. It was a happy but very emotional occasion, made all the more poignant when we discovered that the house mother was also called Anna. It was an extraordinary coincidence. The home is called 'Casa Anna'.

While we were in Romania on this visit we went to see the home near the Birsana Monastery. Now completed, ten girls of various ages, including a few Roma children, had moved in. The children seemed very happy to be living in a real home at last and with house parents who loved and cared for them.

The following year our Romanian team discovered that the Mother Superior had 'thrown out' the Roma children as she said they were not 'good' children. Some time later, we found out that all of the children had been sent away and the house was being used as a 'motel' for paying guests visiting the monastery. We still feel very cheated and upset that the Mother Superior had done such a thing and we suspect that this had been her motive all along. She was not the person we thought she was.

Casa Anna – Anna's Home

Georgette, Delia and Stefan recruited an amazing team of local people. Together they worked tirelessly, seven days a week and often late into the night, to 'rescue' – and if you had seen the conditions they existed in, 'rescue' is the right word – all of the children in the Camin Spital. They

Girls in Anna's Home sharing their cakes

had to carry out painstaking research into the background of every child and find out where they came from and contact their families where possible. At the same time they started to prepare the children for their new life. This was incredibly time-consuming and sensitive work. Many of the children in the Camin Spital had not been outside the building for years. Many of them had never stood on grass or felt the warmth of the sun. Others had seldom been out of their cots and could not stand up because their limbs were so wasted. Silent and with staring eyes, many of them just rocked back and forth and were in a world of their own. In frustration some children banged their heads against the bars of their cots; a few of them had bandages, looking like helmets, wrapped round their heads to protect them. Most children were frightened about the future. This fear was exacerbated sometimes by the staff telling them horror stories of what was to come.

The mental and physical state of every child was analysed by Delia and her team and treatment started. Working with these children hour after hour was emotionally and physically draining. We have the greatest respect and admiration for those staff and volunteers – including Kerry Hall – who gave so much of themselves to these children. Over the months and years that followed, the Romanian team performed miracles and some children who had never walked before, took their first steps, and some who had never spoken began to speak. They discovered that some of the older children, who were very small and still in cots, were, in fact, in their 20s. To us this was unbelievable.

Kerry working with a teenage boy in the Camin Spital

A number of the children were reintegrated with their biological families; for those for whom this was not possible we had to buy or build houses in the surrounding towns and villages. Prior to moving each group of children out of the institution, a great deal of time was spent preparing them psychologically for what was to be a massive change in their lives, particularly for those children who were going back to their families. In many cases they had not seen their family members for many years. They needed help to adjust and so did their family. Obviously they could not just be taken back and left at the front door.

We were very lucky to be present for one reunion when two teenage brothers from the Camin Spital met their birth parents for the first time since they had been taken away by the regime and placed in an orphanage when they were small children. The tears of emotion, the tension, the hugging, touching and laughing were unforgettable. The family visited the two boys on several occasions. Each visit grew longer. Then, one day, the boys were taken to the village for a short visit to the family home. Later they spent one night and then a weekend with their family. Eventually our team thought the time was right for them to go and live with their birth parents. Everyone was happy. Had we not got those two brothers out of the Camin Spital, they would have spent the rest of their lives in an adult mental institution.

One of the children in the Camin Spital was a teenage girl, Anna Maria, whose head was the size of a large beach ball. She lay motionless in her bed. She had hydrocephalus (water on the brain) and was blind and thought to be totally deaf. Although she was being kept alive, she was considered by the doctor and staff in the institution as an 'incuperable'; her only escape from the unimaginable misery of her situation was death. No effort had been made to give her any quality of life whatsoever.

Our team, quickly realising that she could hear certain things, bought a small tape recorder which they put on a table by her head. It was a joy to see her face light up when the music played. Over the course of the next few months individual care plans were developed for all the children to get them out of the hell in which they were existing. In Anna Maria's case it was decided that she should be moved into a small home which was being developed for children with severe special needs. The 'doctor' in the Camin Spital and many of the staff were very angry about this as they were convinced that the move would kill her and we would be guilty of her murder.

Very carefully Anna Maria was moved into her new home and, as it was evident that she could react to light and darkness, a big bed was made for her and placed by a large window. With the loving personal care of the specially-selected staff, and the extra stimulation of the other nine children, as well as being able to smell the food cooking in the kitchen, Anna Maria flourished and her quality of life improved immeasurably.

On his last visit to Romania, Mark went to see Anna Maria. It was obvious that she was much happier – she had a serene smile on her face – and she was more aware of what was going on around her. As Mark was saying goodbye to her, she felt for his hand, took it to her mouth and kissed it gently. Totally overcome Mark rushed outside into the garden and cried.

On a previous visit to Romania Mark went to see one of our newly-opened homes near Sighet. When he arrived he found ten teenage children, smartly dressed, waiting to meet him at the garden gate. The most 'senior' boy called Adi had spent his whole life in institutions. Without saying a word he took Mark's hand, led him up to the front door, opened it and then said in a very serious voice, *"Home."* That one word meant the world to him. For Mark it was another one of those unforgettable moments which made everything worthwhile.

While our HHC Romania team was getting children out of the institutions, we also needed to prevent others from being moved in. We began to introduce new systems and facilities to help vulnerable families and children living at home. These included Day Care Centres where a single parent could leave a child while they were at work; Emergency Reception Centres with caring staff, for families or children while a solution was being found for their problems; and Mother and Baby Units to enable vulnerable young girls to bond with their babies and keep them. The reform of the childcare system in general, including preventing separation, fostering and adoption services, continues today.

We were fortunate that Romania wanted to join the EU; one of the prerequisites to their accession was that they had to close down their institutions and reform their childcare system. This was strongly enforced by the MEP rapporteur, Baroness Emma Nicholson, who became a great advocate of our work. The problem was that this had never been done before, so no-one knew how to do it. For instance, there was one dreadful place called Ocna Şugatag near Sighet where there were over 100 children between 7–17 years old in a huge building. The authorities constructed walls inside and created small apartments, then proudly announced that they had closed the orphanage. In fact, all they had done was to create ghettos. We knew that within them there were some terrible incidences of abuse. When one teenage girl died no-one was held to account.

We were also extremely fortunate that Absolute Return for Kids (ARK), founded by Arpad (Arki) Busson and a group of very successful people in the hedge fund industry in 2001, heard about our work in Romania. Mark and James Whiting had a meeting with a few members of their Board and were grilled about facts and figures. Shortly afterwards Ian Wace, one of the founders, flew out to Romania with Mark and Georgette, in a private jet, to visit our programme and assess the validity of what we had told them.

We flew straight into the very small airport of Satu Mare in the north of the country, in the county of Maramureş in which most of our work was taking place and immediately went straight to an horrendous orphanage. The quick transition from leaving England in the luxury of the jet to arriving at an appalling institution somehow made it particularly shocking. The flight was so quick that it made the differences between the two worlds seem particularly stark.

Knowing that we were only going to be in the country for 24 hours, we arranged a full Saturday/Sunday programme of visits so that Ian could see and experience as much as possible. However, on the Sunday morning, after going to yet another dreadful place, Ian decided he had seen enough and wanted to fly back early so Mark went to the hotel and told the two pilots who were having a lie-in. They got up quickly and went to the airport. We followed shortly afterwards. The airport was deserted, except for a security guard, as they were not expecting any flights that day except our own departure at 4.00pm. On arrival the guard told us that we could not take off until the person from the security department had stamped our passports and he was coming from Cluj, two hours' journey away, specially to do this. There was nothing we could do but wait and wait. Eventually we heard the spluttering of a very old car approaching and the all-important person arrived. Apparently, even if you have a private jet waiting for you on the runway, the man with the rubber stamp has the greater power!

Fortunately Ian was suitably impressed and very moved by what he had experienced and the Board of ARK agreed to start supporting our programme. Without doubt the huge investment of over £11 million that ARK has made in our Romanian programme since 2002 has been critical to its success. Because of their continuing commitment we have been able to plan and expand our whole operation and maintain the momentum. While ARK has been extremely generous with its financial support, at the same time their Board members have been very demanding and rigorous in their scrutiny of our finances and results. This has proved to be an important learning process for us and has made us acutely aware of the necessity for accurate monitoring and evaluation processes for all our programmes.

Arki Busson went out to Romania with the film director Sam Taylor-Johnson, who is one of our Patrons, to see the programme for himself. The visit had a huge impact on both of them. Arki also became a Patron and is still one of

our most committed and passionate supporters. Sam admitted later that she could not sleep well for a long time after she got back, as she had constant flashbacks of the tragic children she had seen.

Our Patrons Sam and Arki

Our Patron Mrs Lily Safra

Not long after this visit Sam and her first husband, Jay Jopling, hosted an evening reception in their lovely London home and many well-known and extremely successful people attended. Amongst these was one of the world's great philanthropists, Mrs Lily Safra, the widow of the very successful and highly respected banker, J. Edmund Safra. During the course of the evening Mark had a long talk with Mrs Safra, but felt that he was not really connecting with her; then along came Sarah Bates (one of our young fundraising staff) and joined in. Mrs Safra was clearly impressed by her and Sarah succeeded in winning her over to our cause. Ever since then Mrs Safra and the Foundation, which she started in memory of her husband, have been the most generous, committed supporters of our work in Romania. On many occasions Mrs Safra has enquired quite spontaneously about the welfare of the children, and at special times, such as when she heard that conditions in Romania were

Sarah Bates (now Whiting)

particularly cold, she made sure that the children received some extra warm clothing. She also gave them other big treats including summer holidays; these were over and above her major funding of new homes.

It seemed that we were in the right place at the right time and our team in Romania had already demonstrated what could be done and how best to do it.

In turn it led to a strong commitment to training social services staff, enabling the authorities and different groups of social workers from other regions in the country to learn from our example. We converted an old electricity power station in Baia Mare into a training centre and it also became our HHC Head Office in Romania. Numerous courses are run there, not only for Romanians, but for many people from other countries who come to see our work

Our Patron Lady Jopling

and learn from our experience. One of these was a delegation of 11 people from Khartoum in Sudan, led by the Minister of State for Social Affairs; they spent eight days working with our team.

Life was not all plain sailing for our team however. They faced enormous challenges including threats, corruption, ignorance and inertia. International adoption had become big business; the US Embassy even had a large staff devoted to this to help their citizens adopt Romanian babies. It was also big money and many Government officials were benefitting from the system. Children were sold abroad for about US $10,000, very often without the adoption going through all the official checking procedures, so it was impossible to know where the children went. We had one awful experience of this when, early one morning, a smart black car arrived at one of our homes. Two men marched in waving papers, saying that they had permission to collect a brother and sister for adoption. The children and staff were screaming with fear as the children were stripped and new clothes put on them. Terrified, they tried to hold on to their carers and clung to bits of furniture in an attempt to resist being taken away, but to no avail. They were bundled into the car and it sped off. We learned later that the siblings had been separated and sent to different countries but no-one knew where they went. We were in Bucharest at the time and personally reported what had happened to the British Ambassador who told us that he was powerless to intervene.

A very bright, young British lawyer, Matt Waldman, was working for us in Romania and Emma Nicholson asked us if we would loan him to her office to help draft new legislation to stop international adoption. As in every country, there were many local families who, for various reasons, wanted to adopt children, but the number of bureaucratic hurdles made it difficult for them to do so. This was partly due to the fact that there was no money in it for those who controlled the fate of these vulnerable children. Much to the anger of many people who were benefitting financially from the system, international adoption was stopped in Romania in 2005.

Adoption is also viewed by many cultures as an admittance of failure that some families are not able to produce their own children – as a result it is considered a shameful stigma. Our aim is to make fostering and adoption within all countries something that a family can be proud of and in no way ashamed. The International Convention on the Rights of the Child states very clearly that international adoption should be the last option for a child, and, wherever possible, children should be brought up in their country of origin.

Dorina, one of the little girls from Cavnic, looking out of a Wendy House. Her eyes were 'dead' when we found her, but now they sparkle

Children with special needs and Roma children are the most difficult to place in countries struggling to cope with limited resources.

Mark went out to Romania in 2010 with the Vice President and Director of the Conrad N. Hilton Humanitarian Prize, Judy Miller, who had asked to see our programme in the country. Just before we arrived, our team had uncovered the terrible case of a young man called Ghita. One afternoon we met Ghita and his girlfriend, Tery, in Stefan's office and they told us their painful story in a quiet, gentle manner with no trace of anger or bitterness.

Due to poverty and pressure from the authorities Ghita's parents had left him against their will in the hospital maternity ward after he was born. Two years later they were still so upset that they decided they had to take him back. Convincing the authorities they were now able to look after him,

A special moment

they were given permission to go and collect him. As he grew up he became increasingly badly behaved and went to prison. His mother always thought there was something strange about him. A few weeks after she died our team discovered what had happened. The parents had been given the wrong boy. Their own son Ghita had spent 26 years in institutional care as a result. He was moved from the hospital to a baby institution, then to an institution for young children and finally, at the age of six, to another institution where he remained until he was a young adult. From there he moved into a male hostel and Tery, who had been with him in the institution, went to a female hostel. Matters were made worse because the man bearing his identity had a criminal record and so no-one would employ the real Ghita. It took months to sort out this bureaucratic nonsense .

Mark was yet again so overcome by this tragic story that he had to leave the room quickly. He asked Stefan to rent an apartment immediately for Ghita and Tery so that they could start a new life together and they are now happily married.

Following Judy's visit, the Conrad N. Hilton Humanitarian Prize sent us an award of US $100,000 in recognition of our work in Romania and all the other countries in which we were operating.

Early in 2014 Ghita was invited to speak at a meeting in the European Parliament in Brussels about his experience during which he said, *"Now that I am older I understand better what we were missing. What was really terrible about institutional care? It was having nowhere to belong, and no-one to belong to – no-one to love."*

Today, despite all of our work in Romania, 9,000 children still remain in institutions and our goal is to close all of them within the next six years. We can understand why some people may wonder why it is taking so long. We know only too well that every day in an institution for a child is one day too long, but finding alternative family care for every single child, and at the same time preventing the abandonment of more children, is a very complex, sensitive and time-consuming task. It cannot be rushed, not least because many of those who remain in institutions have severe special needs.

We could not have achieved so much in Romania without the cooperation and partnership with the Government and local authorities. Those who were reluctant at first to cooperate with us had to be won over. It is obvious that you cannot transform the childcare system of a country unless those in authority want it to happen. All HHC staff everywhere spend a lot of time now in advocating the advantages of family-based rather than institutional care for children. Romania, which inherited a terrible legacy concerning institutionalisation of children from the Ceauşescu era, has become a great example of what, in time, can be achieved.

The Government of Romania is fully committed to reforming its childcare system by supporting family-based care and we are working together with them to close all the remaining institutions in Romania by 2020.

As Stefan said recently, *"We are actually changing the future of millions of children. It will be heaven for them when we do or hell if we don't."*

ॐ

PRIDE AND DETERMINATION
ERITREA

1997 - 2009

The Situation: A 30-year war with Ethiopia ended in May 1991. Out of a population of three million, about 250,000 were killed.

The Problem: Over 50,000 children were orphaned.

Our Initial Plan: To build small homes for children who had no families.

The Outcome: We built six homes and handed over the programme to a local NGO.

"Family is not an important thing – it is everything."
Michael J. Fox

Dr.Tsegai Gherezghiher

> *All of the countries around the Horn of Africa have seen devastating shortages of rain, crops and consequently food over the centuries. Sun-baked and poverty-stricken, Eritrea also suffered 30 years of bitter war with its neighbours, especially with Ethiopia.*

James Whiting, by now an integral member of our small team in the barn, had cycled through Eritrea and spent some time there when on his mammoth bike ride from London to South Africa. He told us of the people's suffering and the plight of many children. He sparked an interest in us. Could we be of help? Once we had made the decision to explore the possibility, it seemed obvious that James was the person to undertake the recce.

In Asmara, the capital, he met a very impressive man called Dr.Tsegai Gherezghiher who had started a local charity called Vision Eritrea to help children. Tsegai had been in the USA throughout the Eritrean war but as soon as it was over he went back. James thought that Vision Eritrea would be the ideal organisation for us to partner.

Shortly afterwards we both went out to see the situation for ourselves. Tsegai met us at the airport and as he was driving us to Asmara, the capital, he happened to mention that he was a Rotarian. We were amazed and delighted. We told him of the wonderful support we were receiving from Rotary International and that Mark had been made an Honorary Rotarian. He couldn't believe it! He told us that his Club was having its first post-war meeting that very evening and he invited us to accompany him. As we arrived they were unwrapping all the Rotary flags, banners and badges which had been carefully packed and hidden away for years. Amongst these was a big sign with '*Rotary Club of Asmara*' written above the Rotary badge and underneath it was written, '*Ethiopia*'. Having just fought a fierce war of independence from Ethiopia, they took great delight in obliterating the word and replacing it with '*Eritrea*'.

The next day Tsegai took us to meet the Minister responsible for Children's Affairs. Many of the senior posts in the Government, including the Minister we met, had fought in the war with Ethiopia; we noticed that Tsegai showed great deference and respect towards them. On arrival we were surprised to find that the Ministry was located in a compound of very smart houses and we were told that they had been built by an international children's charity. Apparently the organisation had contravened building and customs regulations by bringing in materials from Europe, including marble for the stairs. The Government said the charity could no longer be trusted to work in Eritrea, so they had to close their programme, leaving the country and their smart houses behind them.

Bear in charge of the children

Following our meeting with the Minister, Tsegai showed us Asmara and the surrounding area which included a visit to a very attractive new building which turned out to be a baby orphanage. It appeared to be well-run and suitably equipped and we were told that all the children would be reintegrated with their own families or foster families, and then the orphanage would be closed.

As we went round with Tsegai we met various groups of children who Vision Eritrea wanted to help. By chance we came across a man walking beside a long, dusty road and we stopped to talk to him. His name was Mohammed and he was helping Vision Eritrea to trace the families

Bear helping a little boy make his bed ... quite literally

of the children they were supporting. Mohammed was on his way back to Asmara having been walking alone for several weeks in very remote rural areas. He had found family relations of 27 of the children who had become 'lost' during the war. He stood there in his dirty white robes with a small cloth bag on the end of stick over his shoulder, rather like Dick Whittington except he was searching for families not gold. His rugged, lean figure and his quiet dignity and serious determination made a lasting impression on us. Tsegai explained to us how important it was for all children in Eritrea to belong to a family. Without a family it would be difficult, if not impossible, for them to find a husband or wife later on.

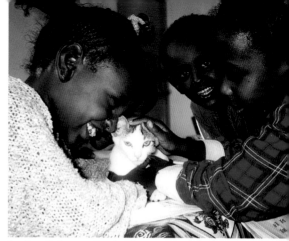

Loving their new family kitten

We were extremely impressed by everyone's determination to rebuild the country. They had great pride and really had no wish to rely on overseas aid. They had won the war and they were now working very hard and positively to establish peace. One of their initiatives concerned teenage youngsters. They were organised to give practical help with various projects including manual labour, such as clearing the bush and building roads, for two weeks every year during their long school holidays.

A family group outside their new home

We were so inspired by the work that Vision Eritrea was doing that we agreed to build five homes for 60 children - 12 in each - in the appropriate localities from which they originated. Work on the houses began, but shortly afterwards in 1998 the building programme was disrupted when the Ethiopian forces invaded Eritrea again. They took over one third of the country, including the areas where three of our houses were being built. In the year 2000, under a UN peace agreement, they withdrew and eventually the homes were completed, giving the children a family-type environment and an education which would ensure their future.

On the way back from Akordat late one evening in Tsegai's 4 x 4, he surprised us by asking if we would like to watch television. He got out a portable set

Posing for the family photo outside their new home

which his son had sent him from the USA and plugged it into the cigarette lighter. We had already had many bizarre experiences and this was yet another one, watching Eritrean television while driving along bumpy roads. Not surprisingly, the reception was very fuzzy!

Tsegai told us that in the area of Barentu there was an abundance of peanuts which he thought could be turned into peanut butter. Not only is it high in protein but, as no-one else in the country was utilising this natural resource, he was making plans to build a factory and all the profits would go towards supporting vulnerable families. This seemed like a brilliant idea. However, he said he would need some cows to produce

Bear hitches a lift

the milk in order to make the butter. That afternoon, he took us to visit a Government farm which had the only remaining herd of Holstein cows. As Caroline grew up on her parents' farm, we were very interested and pleased to see that the cattle were being well cared for. A long discussion about the feasibility of buying some cows, and where and how they would be kept, took place. We became very enthusiastic about this whole idea but did not buy any immediately. This was very lucky since on our return to England we learnt that peanut butter does not contain butter made from milk!

We continued to work with Vision Eritrea until 2009 when Tsegai told us that they were very appreciative of our help, but were now successfully fundraising for themselves and could manage without further support from HHC. We had completed all we set out to achieve since our first visit to Eritrea. We were sad to close our programme there as we really enjoyed working with Tsegai and the lovely Eritrean people. However, this is the outcome we hope for in all countries – that the time will come when each of them no longer needs our support.

෨

TINY GRAVES
SUDAN

1998 -

The Situation: 40 years of intermittent civil conflict has led to a humanitarian crisis.

The Problem: Thousands of children had been displaced and orphaned, many becoming 'street children'.

Our Initial Plan: To create small homes for some of these children.

The Outcome: We created 15 homes and are working with the Government to reform their childcare system.

"Where there is love, there is life."
Mahatma Ghandi

We discovered that there was a baby orphanage in Khartoum called Maygoma which had up to 200 abandoned babies in it at any one time. Most of the babies were abandoned by young, unmarried mothers who, with their babies, were deemed to be regarded as 'sinful' under Sharia law. The police would find the babies, often left on rubbish dumps, as they went on their duty rounds; they would put them in the back of their truck and take them to the orphanage at the end of their shift. By this time some were already dead and others would be suffering from severe dehydration. Conditions in the orphanage were deplorable. Baby milk and food were scarce and of poor quality. The result was that about 85% of the babies who were admitted to the orphanage, died within a month. Outside the back wall was a big open expanse of common ground with numerous small mounds, like molehills. These were the unmarked graves of the babies who had died in the orphanage.

The plight of these and many more children was totally desperate. Great friends of ours who have close links with Sudan had very sadly just lost their youngest son. Harry died in a car accident on his way home from school on 13 March 1996; he was 14 years old. He was the most lovely, popular, funny and talented boy who brought a ray of sunshine to everyone he met. It was a terrible tragedy which profoundly affected all of us who knew him. None of us could realise at that time the impact that his short life would have on thousands of children.

A few weeks after his death we invited his parents, David and Kate Henderson, to supper. We said we would like to do something in Harry's memory and we discussed various ideas. They suggested that it would be very special and appropriate if we could do something to help the children in Sudan. Just two months before Harry died, David and Kate had taken him on a holiday to Egypt. They went on a boat down the Nile towards the border with Sudan and talked a lot about their family connection and their love of the country. David's family has had a very long association with Sudan; his father had been in the British Administration in Sudan and his last post was Governor of the Province of Darfur. David himself had been born there and spent his early childhood in the country. Later he went back to Sudan to teach for two years in the boys' secondary school in El Fasher, the capital of Darfur.

Early in 1998 we made some useful contacts in the country and we asked David if he would go there to carry out a recce; we wanted him, Kate and their son, Alex and daughter, Tessa, to be connected right from the start with any project we might implement. David went out on 12 April and had an extremely full, interesting and constructive visit, meeting numerous people in the Government and other agencies working with children. On his return he wrote very detailed reports with suggestions as to how we might proceed. He highlighted three important factors. First, the strength of the extended family and kinship which had survived the widespread and prolonged disruption caused by war and famine; second, that we should make best use of this social capital and its strengths by reintegrating children with their families whenever possible; the third point was that the childcare agencies he met wanted real partners; one man told him, *"We want partners to understand and share our priorities, not Father Christmases who appear with hand-outs once a year and then disappear."*

Following further discussions with David and armed with his report, Mark went out to Sudan in August 1998 with Norman Jackson. Norman had been Save the Children's Country Director there for several years and was a fluent Arabic speaker. As he knew numerous people in Khartoum and was highly respected, doors opened and everything was made straightforward to plan the way ahead.

We decided to form partnerships with two local organisations, Amal and Sabah, who were working with vulnerable children and were well regarded. We discussed ideas about buying houses for up to ten children in each, with foster parents to look after them. Mark was keen that these family homes should be of mixed tribe and with both boys and girls so that they could learn to live together and understand one another. Norman, however, with his knowledge and experience, rejected this idea explaining that, under Muslim law, boys and girls who were not of the same biological family should not live together. He also suggested that children from the same tribes should be kept together so that they would retain their own language and customs, including songs and dances. Norman said that these skills were extremely important in the hope that one day the children might be able to return to their biological families. This turned out to be very sound advice and was in line with David's original recommendations. The house parents were selected from the same tribe as the children and soon elders of the local community of that tribe took an interest and actively helped them.

On the night of 7 August the Americans launched a cruise missile which destroyed a pharmaceutical factory on the outskirts of Khartoum, explaining that they had evidence that it was developing a nerve gas for use by al-Qaeda. Osama Bin Laden had previously lived in Khartoum in the same street as Norman Jackson, who had seen him occasionally. The world media arrived the next day; the speed with which they set up their equipment was impressive.

The British Ambassador, Alan Goulty, and his wife Lilian, had invited Mark and Norman to dinner the following evening. The next day he telephoned Mark in his hotel. Mark immediately presumed that he was calling to cancel the dinner, but this was not so. The Ambassador explained that the Foreign Secretary wanted to speak to him at 7.00pm and asked us to come a little later. On our arrival the Ambassador told us that he had been instructed to close the Embassy in two days and return to the UK; this was obviously a big shock. However, undaunted and with the 'sangfroid' one would expect from a British Ambassador, he had decided that we should have a party with the best food that they had in the larder and the finest wines. Only two other guests had been invited; they were both Irish Catholic priests and they knew how to party! After an excellent dinner of smoked salmon and fillet steak, with copious glasses of good claret, we went into the drawing room and a bottle of the best malt whisky was produced. One of the priests went over to the piano and started playing. The rest of us gathered round and we all sang patriotic songs and hymns as the good ship Britannia was slowly sinking. It was an extraordinary evening and a great party!

We invited all the key people we had met during our week's visit to lunch on the last day, in a restaurant by the confluence of the Blue and White Niles. It was pouring with rain and the restaurant had a tin roof. About 25 men came (no women), most of them very big and swarthy, including a few plain-clothed policemen who stood at the back keeping a watchful eye on us. For Mark, who had never been to Sudan before, the whole experience was surreal as he looked around the table in amazement, wondering what had

Bear visiting children in their homes

Enjoying a tribal dance in one of the homes

brought him here. He then realised it was all because of Harry. He stood up and banged on the table. As the rain crashed on the roof Mark told everybody about Harry, how his family had very close connections with Sudan and how he had died. He explained that we wanted to create some small homes for the displaced children in his memory. Finally Mark proposed that the homes should all be called Harry's Homes - then he sat down. No-one spoke. Eventually a tall man called Dr. Waleed stood up and said in a clear, deep voice, *"I would further like to propose that all the children in Harry's Homes are called Harry's brothers and sisters."* It was an extraordinarily emotional moment for everyone there as they mumbled their agreement.

Although we planned for Amal and Sabah to buy the houses on our behalf and select the foster parents and the children, we realised that we needed to find someone to oversee the project. In order to do this we had to be given registration by the Sudanese Government to work in the country; this proved to be no easy or quick task. After several months we received registration and appointed a wonderful man called Farid Idris to become our Country Director. Fifteen years later he is still there and we fondly call him our Gentle Giant!

In all we created 15 Harry's Homes for over 100 children in Khartoum and Ombdurman. The children all went to local schools and, like all the other children, became part of the community, forming friendships and visiting one another's houses. It was rewarding to see the transformation in their lives and the way they all grasped the chance to improve their education and prospects. On one visit Mark took Hope Bear who ('who' is appropriate!) was, as always, a great

Farid with Bear

hit with all the children. Whilst visiting one family, two boys took Bear into their bedroom and sat on a bed with him. Out loud they told him their life story. Farid and Mark listened through the half-open door as they explained what had happened to them, how they had been living on the streets, picked up by the police, taken to a prison-like camp and beaten. But now, they said, they had a nice home, went to school and they were very happy.

On the last night of the visit Amal and Sabah organised a big party for all of Harry's families and the children performed their own tribal songs and dances. Everyone had a great time, including Bear who was passed around throughout the evening. Transport was arranged and eventually the families were taken back to their various homes. Then Mark realised that Bear was missing. He had been 'bearnapped'! The staff from Amal and Sabah went round all the homes and eventually found him with two of the girls. They were completely distraught when he was taken from them.

Bear at the big party

In 2004 we were fortunate to be one of the three charities selected by the *Daily Telegraph* for their Christmas Appeal; the others were Medical Relief International (Merlin), and a local housing group. A correspondent went out to Sudan to see our work there. The Appeal started in November and ran until the end of January. Before Christmas we had received quite a lot more money than the other two charities which was pleasing. Then, on 26 December, the catastrophic Asian tsunami struck. The media was saturated with pictures and stories of the epic tragedy. Emotive appeals were made by numerous disaster relief agencies and donations for our work with 'invisible' children almost dried up. On 16 February 2005 Lord Carrington and James came with us to a reception and presentation for the three charities in the office of the Editor of the *Daily Telegraph*. We received a wonderful cheque for £295,000 ... Merlin got one for over £5 million because of their work with the victims of the tsunami.

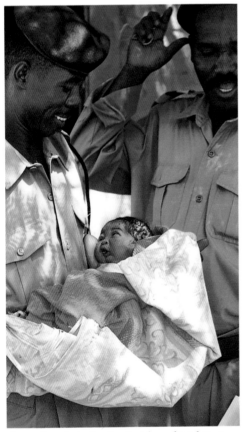

A new-born baby having just been found on a rubbish dump by two policemen

Over the last twenty years many such visible disasters have been given extensive coverage by the media which elicit, quite rightly and understandably, an amazingly generous response. It is so much harder to get that same reaction and support for children who are hidden away in orphanages or orphans of HIV/AIDS trying to survive in child-headed households, all of whom are out of sight and out of mind. Such was the case with the awful Maygoma Institution in Khartoum. Its very existence was largely a secret in the Sudanese capital. Behind its walls, thousands of babies had died over decades of absolute neglect. For us to succeed in ending this nightmare, we had to expose the situation and work with the religious and political leaders.

Farid arranged for Médecins sans Frontières to provide milk for the babies in Maygoma and we provided other assistance including baby food. Next Farid brought the whole dire situation to the attention of the Khartoum State Minister for Social Services, who was a very compassionate and enlightened Muslim cleric. The Minister considered that under Sharia law, the mothers were 'guilty of sin', but the babies were not. He told the police to actually look for the abandoned babies and take them immediately to the orphanage and try to save their lives. The result was that the mortality rate was cut dramatically, but this created another problem – there were even more orphaned babies to care for.

We arranged for Farid to take the Minister and nine members of his staff to visit our programme in Romania, where they spent a week studying all aspects of our work and our model of childcare reform. Having been slightly sceptical and questioning on arrival, they certainly were not by the end of the visit. On the last night the Sudanese Ambassador in Bucharest gave a party in his residence. He had personally telephoned us, insisting that we fly out for it, saying that his car would meet us at the airport. It was a great party, and in a speech of thanks the Minister said he was determined to reform the Khartoum State system along the lines of our work that he had seen in Romania.

Georgette flew out from Romania to Sudan shortly afterwards to help Farid plan this reformation. One of the first things they had to do was to address the problem of the ever-increasing number of babies who were surviving. They organised a media campaign to explain the situation and invited people to become foster parents. This was a completely new concept, but the result was astonishing. Hundreds of people applied to foster a child from the orphanage. They were all interviewed and checks made on suitability; following this, childcare training was organised for those selected by our small team and local officials. Some wanted to be long-term, life-long foster parents similar to full adoption, which is not normal under Sharia law; others wanted to be emergency, short-term foster parents giving their love to children while their futures were determined.

We went out to witness the day when the first 20 mothers came to the orphanage to collect their babies. There was a great sense of nervous excitement as they arrived, clearly dressed in their finest, bright toabs. An awning had been

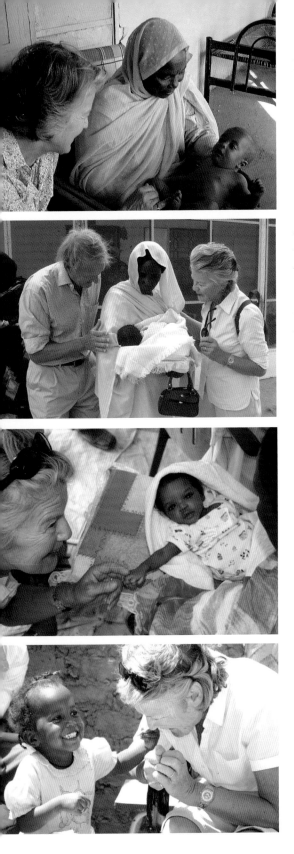

put up in the grounds for shade and there were white plastic chairs for everyone to sit on. First of all each mother was given her 'starter pack' of a plastic bath, nappies, soap, powder, milk and clothes. The excitement increased. Then the orphanage staff came out of the building and gave each mother their tiny, new baby. We watched as one young mother, in a bright red toab, took her baby in her two hands and just looked at her in wonder; then she started talking to her. Farid was listening with us as she explained to her baby that she was going to love and look after her for the rest of her life. Lifting the baby up to her face she said, *"You smell like honey."*

We were delighted by the amazingly positive response of the Sudanese to this pioneering initiative. In the year 2006 we placed 790 children with new families and prevented the abandonment of a further 119. Since then we estimate that over 2,000 babies have been placed with families. Had HHC not started working in Sudan, the majority of them would have died.

The next step was to try and prevent the abandonment of babies in the first place. Farid and his team worked hard with the State authorities to develop ways to do this. Amongst these was the concept of having a

A very happy foster mother 'and her son' after a year together

social worker in each maternity hospital and training them and the medical staff to look out for vulnerable mothers and help them to keep their children where possible, or arrange for them to be put into foster care rather than the orphanage.

We were hoping to close Maygoma within a few years, but unfortunately the enlightened and supportive Minister in Khartoum was moved to another post and replaced by a woman who could not see the necessity for reforming the system. Even so, conditions in the orphanage had been vastly improved for the new arrivals. The mortality rates had dropped dramatically and fostering had become an established system for giving numerous children a future.

In January 2005 a peace agreement was signed in Sudan ending the 20 year civil war which had resulted in 1.5 million deaths and an estimated 200,000 children becoming orphans. Many of the children in Harry's Homes came from the South and the Nuba mountains originally, so this meant they could return to their homes if it was possible, but only if they wanted to. Obviously this had to be thought about very carefully and sensitively by everyone involved and it had to include the children themselves. Our team in Khartoum developed a project to establish a set of principles in conjunction with the children and the

Tessa and her camera captivating the children

young adults to help them make up their own minds as to what they wanted to do. The project, which we called *'When Peace Comes'*, got the support of the UK Department for International Development which allocated £500,000 to us over four years in order to carry this out.

Gail Jopling

Fifteen children and young adults from our homes canvassed opinions and acted as the voice of hundreds of children who were living in Khartoum away from their families. With the assistance of our team, they carried out questionnaires and held meetings where they used drawings, story-telling, poetry and songs to help gain a true understanding of the situation faced by the children if they went home. This proved to be a great success and in the first year 50 children rejoined their families and many more followed.

David, Farid, Alex, Tessa and Kate at one of Harry's Homes

At the beginning of 2013 we expanded our work in the country and are now working with the Government to implement their national policy across nine separate States including White Nile and Gezira. This project will focus on preventing child abandonment, replacing institutional care with emergency and long-term family-based care, reuniting babies with their mothers and recruiting foster carers and potential adoptive parents. By providing social workers and the police with better solutions for vulnerable children and removing the reliance on institutional care we aim to have a lasting impact on childcare across Sudan and neighbouring countries.

David and Kate Henderson went to Sudan in 2003 and then again in 2006 with Alex and Tessa. Tessa went back there for six weeks in 2008 to work with our team and do research for her degree. A report by David and Kate follows. (Their comments about the compassion and care of our Sudan team, and the quality of their work, applies equally to all our overseas programmes.)

None of this would have happened had Harry not died. He saved the lives of thousands of children. For us personally, Harry's story is the most extraordinary and inspiring occurrence in the first 20 years of HHC.

୬

OUR VISITS TO HHC IN KHARTOUM
JANUARY 2003 AND JANUARY 2006

There is an affinity between people from Britain and the majority of Sudanese, regardless of where they come from in that vast country, which tends to become self-evident very quickly whenever they meet. This happened to us on our two visits to Hope and Homes for Children in Khartoum, and we left with clear impressions of, and immense respect for:

The team's determination to confront and turn round daunting, entrenched convictions and practices concerning: responses appropriate to the needs of street children, of abandoned babies and of unmarried mothers; the disadvantages of custodial care in large institutions compared with the advantages of creating family life in small foster homes; and the acceptability, or otherwise, of fostering and adoption.

The quality of the crucial relationships and range of contacts they had built up with other like-minded government and non-government professionals working in the field of caring for these vulnerable, very young children.

The meticulous investigations they conducted into each locality when the homes were being set up to ensure that the neighbours would be friendly and sympathetic, the local schools would be welcoming and supportive, and the locality itself was appropriate.

Their careful selection of foster parents with the particular strengths needed to create and maintain a genuine family atmosphere in the homes; their routine of visits made every week to each home to confirm that all was well with each child, and to ensure that the children knew and trusted someone other than their foster parents to turn to if they needed alternative help and support.

The painstaking procedures the team followed to go into the tribal background of each child, search for close or extended family, and then establish and sustain these connections so central to personal identity and sense of self-worth amongst the Sudanese.

And it is only right that we should finish by stating that, during our conversations with people in various Sudanese NGOs, it was made very clear to us that they had a great respect for the way Hope and Homes for Children had gone about establishing itself in Khartoum and finding out from them how it could be of use. And they also referred to Farid Idris with considerable respect. They had much admiration for the tactful but persistent diplomacy with which he had handled some serious difficulties, and for the effectiveness of the team he had put together. Above all, they hold him in high regard for the profound changes he has achieved with his team in so many aspects of the care of abandoned babies and of destitute street children in Sudan. For us there could not possibly be a more fitting memorial to our beloved son Harry.

Kate & David

Kate and David Henderson

❧

Kate and David

CHALLENGING TIMES
UKRAINE

1998 -

The Situation: In 1991 Ukraine became independent from the Soviet Union with the legacy of poverty and high unemployment.

The Problem: Over 100,000 children existed on the streets and in various types of institutions.

Our Initial Plan: To provide homes for some of the children.

The Outcome: 65 homes were created and we continue to work with the Government to reform their childcare system.

"Being deeply loved by someone gives you strength,
while loving someone deeply gives you courage."
Lau Tzu

> *One night I met a group of street children who 'existed' in a public park. In the gloom I saw one little girl beating a comatose man on a bench with her fists as she sobbed and screamed at him. The man was her alcoholic father and she was crying out, "Why, why, why?" Many of these children had dogs which they obviously loved and the dogs loved them in return. It was, possibly, the only love that they would ever experience.* (Mark)

Bohdan Rymarenko, our volunteer International Coordinator, was born in Ukraine and although living abroad for much of his life, he has always maintained close links with the country. On 15 February 1998 he received a telephone call from the Ukrainian Minister for Family and Youth, Mrs Valentyna Dovzhenko, asking to meet him. He immediately called us and we told him to go to Ukraine.

The Minister explained that they had started a programme to find homes for vulnerable children but needed help in developing it. This entailed building or buying houses for established families who would then take in at least five children from orphanages. One of the parents would be given the salary of a teacher and an allowance for each child. The Minister wanted us to fund some houses. She explained that the local

Mark and Bohdan (right) briefing the British Ambassador and First Secretary

authority would own the houses and that ownership would be transferred to the family if they were still together after 15 years. This seemed like a very good idea to us as it meant that we would be rescuing children from orphanages and giving them the love of a family and the chance of a positive future for a relatively small outlay.

Mark flew out to Kiev to meet the Minister with Bohdan and sign a MOU to build six houses initially in various villages outside Kiev. Ukraine had become well-known because of the Chernobyl nuclear disaster in 1986. Mark asked the Minister if it would be possible for them to visit the power station. The Minister agreed and arranged a visit for the following day. A car collected the two of us from the old Soviet-style hotel that they had put us in and we drove north out of Kiev. Some 60 miles before we reached Chernobyl we were stopped by guards at the edge of the contaminated zone. On showing them our authorisation papers we were allowed to drive along the deserted road to the power station where we were met by a senior member of staff.

A sarcophagus had been constructed over the reactor which had exploded, but there was still one reactor working. We had to put on special protective clothing for our tour around the plant. After the visit we were invited to lunch in the workers' canteen. The greasy and watery potato soup and bread was, we agreed, definitely the worst lunch we had ever had. We felt extremely sorry for the people who were still working in such an unbelievably awful environment.

After lunch we were taken to Pripyat, a city five miles away. It had been home to 50,000 people - many of whom worked in the power station - and their families. A few days after the explosion, on 26 April 1986, they were suddenly given a few hours in which to leave. All these years later it was exactly as it had been but without people – it was, quite literally, a ghost town. We found it an extremely eerie experience.

Building one of our first homes - for £15,000!

Being astute, Bohdan suggested that £15,000 should be HHC's maximum contribution towards the cost of each house in Ukraine. It was agreed that the local authority, the community and each family should cover the remaining costs either by raising the extra funding or by carrying out the physical work on a voluntary basis. The result was that some really nice family-sized houses were built. The families and communities took great pride in what they had created for some of the children from orphanages

– they had given them a new life and the families a house large enough for everyone.

The first six houses were funded by St. James's Place (SJP), one of our major corporate supporters. Five members of their Foundation Committee, with their Chairman, Malcolm Cooper-Smith, went out for the opening of the first two family homes. Opening ceremonies were very special occasions attended by local and State dignitaries and members of the community. There were always speeches and a ceremonial presentation of a very large and beautiful loaf of bread accompanied by some salt - a national tradition - and, of course, numerous toasts with vodka.

Halya with a mother and foster child

In 1999 we decided that we needed a permanent presence in the country since Bohdan was only able to make flying visits to Ukraine from time to time. Our first task was to establish a small office in Kiev. Luckily for us Halya Postoliuk, who was on the personal staff of Mrs Dovzhenko, agreed to become our first Country Director; thankfully for us Halya is still in post. Thanks to the great support we received from the Minister herself, the commitment of Bohdan and the enthusiasm, energy and efficiency of Halya, the programme developed at an astonishing pace. In the first two years we created 40 family homes in 9 oblasts ('counties') for 460 children. In all we funded 65 homes for over 700 children; Mark visited most of them with Halya and her very small, dedicated staff team.

Although it was great to be able to give so many children a new life in a real, loving family, we realised that this was not going to solve the problem for an ever-increasing number of children being abandoned. The main causes of this were unemployment and poverty, exacerbated by the break-

up of the Soviet Union in 1991. For many parents under stress this led to an increasing dependence on vodka to dull their misery and the feeling of hopelessness. As a result there are numerous street children in Kiev. It gets desperately cold in the winter and many of them exist in the underground sewage system in their search for warmth and security. In order to assuage their misery, hunger and suffering, most resort to sniffing glue. One night Mark went out with a local man, Alexander, who had started an NGO working with the street children; he was horrified by what he saw. The plight of these poor homeless children was desperate.

Carrying ceremonial loaves of bread at the opening of a home

Earlier that day Mark had been to the opening of another of our homes and, as always, been presented with a beautifully decorated large loaf of bread. He had taken this with him in a plastic bag as he thought the street children might like it. When he took it out, the children passed it round, smelling it with exclamations of pleasure. Mark then 'broke the bread' in pieces and gave them to the children who, in turn, broke their piece and gave half to their dogs. The children then asked Mark if he wanted to see where they slept. They led him in the darkness through the park. He could smell the place long before he saw it – they were sleeping

Meeting one of our new families at an opening ceremony

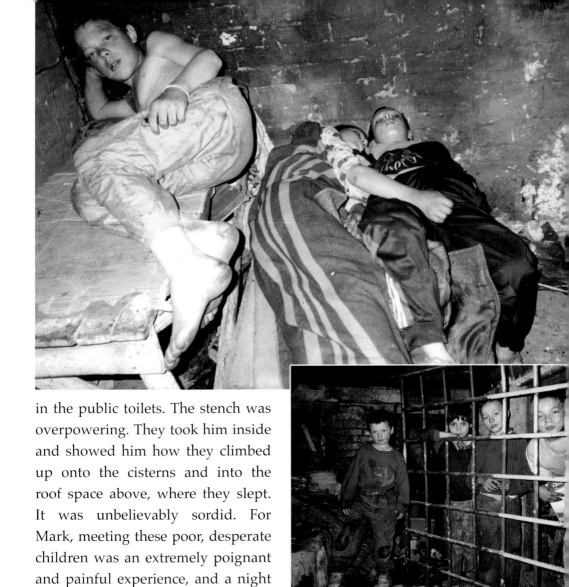

in the public toilets. The stench was overpowering. They took him inside and showed him how they climbed up onto the cisterns and into the roof space above, where they slept. It was unbelievably sordid. For Mark, meeting these poor, desperate children was an extremely poignant and painful experience, and a night he will never forget.

Home - in the sewers

It was estimated that there were 103,000 children orphaned or deprived of parental care at the time and each year subsequently 20,000 children were being placed in orphanages. We had to start addressing the cause of this disaster and prevent further abandonment. As so often is the case, teenage girls were amongst the most vulnerable. One of the first, small but very significant steps was to help these young girls to keep their babies. We developed the first ever Mother and Baby Unit in Ukraine in a town called Kherson in Odessa. This was funded by Martin Rashdi, an SJP Partner, and his wife, Anna, and is called *'The Summer Hope Rashdi Home'* in memory of their daughter who died just nine hours after she was born.

Some of our families

Our aim was to provide a place where the young mothers could live while they bonded with their babies and a plan for their future independence could be worked out. It proved to be very successful and we developed another at Fastiv near Kiev. The Government was so impressed by these units that in 2008 legislation ensured that they became part of the statutory childcare service. We helped the Government create 17 new units following our model, preventing the abandonment of 578 children the following year.

Ukraine encourages and respects large families and any number of up to 10 or 12 children is not uncommon. The mother of the first home we opened was actually given a medal by the President, personally, for being a model parent of such a large family. Many of the parents who took children from orphanages had their own biological children. It was very normal for a whole family to decide to share their love with other children who had none. So you could go into a family home with ten children, some being birth children and others from an orphanage, and be unable to detect the difference between them. We certainly never asked who was who while the children were within earshot.

The growing, rearing, storing, pickling, cooking and eating of food plays a major role in the bonding of these families. It is also common practice for the whole family to sit down at the kitchen table and eat meals together – something perhaps we, in this country, could learn from. We have never seen a 'takeaway' meal being eaten there in front of the 'telly'! They are truly inspirational people. The genuine love we felt when we visited these families always moved us; it was very powerful. The parents were amazing in their total dedication to all the children – often they were unable even to take a break or have a holiday.

In 2003 Halya arranged a very special event to celebrate the fifth birthday of our work in Ukraine. She organised a two-week holiday in a Government resort on the Black Sea coast near Odessa, to which all the children from our 65 homes were invited. In the first week they were on their own and they were joined by their 'parents' for the second week. It was an extremely complex, logistical challenge for our small team; they

had to get everybody there from remote villages all over Ukraine by bus and train, as well as organising their accommodation, food and entertainment for two weeks. The children had a wonderful time. The numerous activities included competitions, shows, dances, swimming and building sand castles. Many had never seen the sea before. Different families met for the first time and experiences were shared and new friendships made. Mark spent the first week with the children and Bohdan joined the families for the second. It was a truly happy and memorable time for everyone there ... Mark included.

Everyone old enough remembers the shocking pictures of the children in orphanages in Romania when Ceauşescu was overthrown – the humanitarian response was fantastic, if not always well-directed. But when the media moves on from one crisis to the next, the world quickly forgets the previous crises. This has always posed a dilemma for us, namely how to make people aware of the continuing suffering of children hidden away in institutions. Every disaster puts them back at the bottom of the priority list – at the end of the 'bread queue'.

Rick Foulsham (our CEO 2006-2011) in one of our homes in Ukraine

Since HHC began we have taken many people out to visit our programmes and they never fail to be shocked by the plight of the children and impressed by our work. Seeing really is believing and the worse the conditions the greater the response from our supporters. But we really regret the need to 'exhibit' these children in such an insensitive and voyeuristic way. It seems repugnant. Some of the institutions for children in which we have worked in Romania have been far more horrifying than in any other country and, as a result, the financial support to rescue them has been easier to obtain. Mark mentioned this to Halya one day in Ukraine and told her to take the next party of visitors to some of the worst institutions in the country (similar to those in Romania), to make them really understand the need. Halya responded rather indignantly by asking if there was now a competition between countries to show off the worst orphanages!

There is another aspect to this dilemma. The authorities in the countries that have these dreadful places want to keep them hidden from the world. We need to expose them to get them closed. When we have done so it has often caused a problem for our teams and set back their work in the country; this has happened on several occasions. We have learnt that it is vital to work closely with the Government and local authorities in each country and be aware of their sensitivities. Our Country Directors face many and varied challenges; some are common to them all, such as never having a big enough budget to do everything they would like to do. This is extremely frustrating for them.

One of the major challenges for our team in Ukraine has been the constant instability of the Government over the last 20 years. There is no civil service as we know it in this country, so when the Government changes, everyone working in the various departments also changes; there is no continuity. It's rather like *Snakes and Ladders*! We were lucky when we began our work that Mrs Dovzhenko was such a great believer in the importance of families for children. She was also a good friend of the President, Leonid Kucma, and his wife who took a keen interest in our work. Mark had a personal audience with the President when he was awarded the decoration of Yaroslav the Wise! Halya, too, was given the award of the Order of Princess Olga. But soon after this event the Government changed and with it the old Ministry which became the State Committee on Youth Policy, Sport and Tourism, with no mention of children. We went to meet the new Minister who was very keen on sport, particularly boxing and the next Olympic Games; unfortunately he regarded the welfare of children as a lower priority. Since then there have been many changes in the name of the Ministry and the people running it.

Sting   *Photo by Alexander Glyadyelov*

Sting, the world-famous singer, went to Kiev to give a concert and he agreed to come and open one of our homes. Mrs Kucma also decided to attend. Torrential rain poured down as we all waited, under our umbrellas, for them to arrive. Mrs Kucma came first with the wailing sirens and flashing lights of a large police escort. Sting arrived about five minutes later with even more noise and commotion. Both were surrounded by a phalanx of very large men in mackintoshes. Mark gave one of the young girls who, until a week earlier, had been living in a sewer, an HHC badge to pin to Sting's coat during the opening ceremony. As she couldn't reach up to him, Sting, completely naturally, went down on one knee in a position of supplication. It was an extraordinarily symbolic moment.

Unlike Romania, which had to transform its childcare system in order to join the European Union, there was not the same imperative for the Ukrainian authorities to change their old, institutionalised system. In fact Halya initially told us never to mention the word 'deinstitutionalisation' for fear of antagonising the authorities and possibly losing their support for our work. But gradually we started talking about it and in 2008 Halya decided that the time was right to open up the debate. In October she organised a two-day conference in partnership with UNICEF, in Kiev, which was attended by over 200 people working in children's services throughout Ukraine. Mark and Delia both attended the conference and spoke. At the start of the two days there were many opponents and sceptics, but by the end there were very few who could not see the merit of reforming the country's system. It was a big breakthrough.

In May 2008 we signed an agreement with the Ministry to close the first institution in Ukraine at Barvinok, near Makariv, about one hour from Kiev. There were about 50 children aged 3–18 years in the institution. The Director and staff were extremely hostile to the plan to close it; they even spread fear amongst the children by telling them that they would be abandoned and far worse off if it happened. A major part of this closure project was the creation of a new Centre to bring all the various departments concerned with childrens' welfare, such as health, education and social services, under one roof. Unfortunately there was no suitable building in the area which we could convert for this use, so this meant we had to start from scratch and create something from nothing. A daunting task. The local authority gave us a really

scrubby piece of land, amongst the run-down houses, on which we built the Centre; it included a Mother and Baby Unit and Emergency Reception area and Daycare Unit. On the same site we built a home for 12 children. It was an enormous challenge for our team and particularly for Nadia, Halya's deputy, who managed the project. A local architect drew up plans and estimated the cost would be just over £1 million! How were we going to raise such a vast sum? Luckily 'the cavalry' arrived just in the nick of time.

David Bellamy, the CEO of SJP, came to visit us in our office at short notice one afternoon. We told him about

David Bellamy inspecting his Ukrainian cavalry on a visit to look at the project

the project and he immediately said that he would ask their Foundation Committee to agree to fund the whole project. Thankfully the Committee approved his incredibly generous proposal. This was a great relief for all of us as it meant we had a firm commitment right through to completion. We could proceed with confidence.

The mountain of paperwork and bureaucracy increased daily. Numerous Ministries became involved; some of the officials used threats, coercion and bribery. In spite of all the obstacles the whole project was completed on time and with only a very small overspend – this was an amazing achievement.

In October 2011 the new Centre, named 'Ray of Hope', was officially opened by the Governor of Kiev Oblast and Malcolm Cooper-Smith, the Chairman of the SJP Foundation.

Numerous people from different parts of Ukraine came to see the new Centre and how it worked. In 2013 alone there were 56 official visits by a total of 800 people, including President Yanakovic in December. Three days after his visit he issued a decree that such centres should be established in every

At the opening of the Ray of Hope Centre

region of Ukraine. This was the highest possible testimony of the quality of the work carried out by Halya and her team over the last 15 years. HHC was having a massive impact on the future of the most vulnerable children in Ukraine, and now the President himself was championing our model of reform. The future looked bright.

Nick Mitchell-Briggs, Mark, Halya, Richard Herbert (SJP) and Malcolm at the opening

How are the mighty fallen? Just a few weeks after his visit the President had to flee his own country by helicopter one night and seek sanctuary in Russia for his own safety. He had been indicted for ordering the killing of many protestors on the streets of Kiev by police snipers. He left behind an enormous ugly house which he had built whilst he was President, costing over £50 million, hidden away in a large area of land outside Kiev. Not for him a moat and a duck pond – he had created a large lake complete with a full-scale pirate ship. Where had the money come from? His own people were, understandably, extremely angry, as were we. For 15 years we had fought for funding to help the children of Ukraine.

Malcolm opening the Ray of Hope Centre with the Governor of the Kiev Oblast

Nadya greeting Maryna Poroschenko, the wife of the new President, to the Centre on 25 June 2014

Despite the turmoil in Ukraine in 2014 Halya and her HHC team continue working tirelessly and with total dedication to reform the childcare system in their country. They deserve many more awards and medals.

༺

Halya with children

Building Together
Belarus

LATVIA

RUSSIA

LITHUANIA

Polatsk
Vitesbk
Hlybokoye

Minsk
Moghilev

BELARUS

Grodno
Gomel

POLAND

Brest

UKRAINE

2000 -

The Situation: A Communist style of dictatorship and an alliance with Russia resulted in severe poverty.

The Problem: Numerous babies and children existed in orphanages.

Our Initial Plan: To create small family homes to rescue some of the children.

The Outcome: 35 homes were created and two institutions closed.

"What was terrible about institutional care? It was having nowhere to belong, and no-one to belong to – no-one to love."

Ghita

The children's big brass band with battered old instruments proudly greeted us as we entered the large, grey Dickensian orphanage. After the official welcome three teenage girls escorted us on a tour of the building. We started in the huge dining room and kitchen; both reeked of boiled cabbage. Then we were taken upstairs into several long dormitories with dozens of beds in each, all looking identical and so immaculate that an army sergeant major would have been pleased. There were no individual lockers or cupboards. None were needed; the children possessed nothing of their own. In the classrooms there were dilapidated desks and a few very old, tattered books. After the tour, Mark thanked the girls and said, "You have a roof over your head, food, a bed and a school - what more do you want?" They looked at him as only teenagers can – with disdain and disbelief – and chorused with one voice, "A family."

Belarus was very badly affected by the Chernobyl explosion in Ukraine on 26 April 1986. The wind took the nuclear fallout from the disaster right over the country. The lives of numerous families and children were devastated as a result. In 1997, three years after HHC began, we asked Bohdan to go to Belarus to see if we could help in any way. He discovered a local organisation, The Belarussian Children's Fund (BCF), which was doing great work and had established a good reputation. Following discussions with Alexander Trukhan, the President of BCF, we decided that our two organisations could work together to get children out of institutions and into small family homes.

Over the next few years our partnership with BCF flourished. We set up 36 homes, many of them funded by SJP. Mark and Bohdan visited most of the families in their homes. As in Ukraine, we never failed to be impressed and uplifted by the love the families gave to the children who they had taken into their homes from the orphanages. Most of the families were large, having several biological children as well as those they were fostering.

One afternoon we went to visit a particularly large, extraordinarily gifted family, named Sentsov, who wanted to move out of their very basic, small wooden house; it was damp, had crumbling walls – and was totally overcrowded. Most of the children had been taken out of the local orphanage. Although the family members were obviously very united and happy, the conditions

14 year old Alexander Sentsov who painted the Christmas card on page 215

in which they were existing were dire. The mother taught them all cooking, needlework, painting and pottery, while the father taught them engineering and carpentry. The parents and children were all incredibly artistic. We sat around in the tiny room which was full of their creative work and were given all sorts of homemade cakes to eat. Then the family said they wanted to perform a short play for us. They all took part and, sadly, it was painfully true to life. It concerned a family who had a lazy, out-of-work, drunken father. The final scene took us by surprise. The man's wife suddenly appeared from the kitchen with a real Kalashnikov rifle and shot him. Fortunately it was not loaded! This dramatic ending to the play was a complete shock to us and took our breath away.

One of our families with Galina (wearing sunglasses)

This enterprising family had identified a large half-finished house which was for sale. As they were teetering on the brink of disaster, and it was very cheap, on impulse we decided to buy it for them. The whole family set to work on completing the building; they made it into a really spacious, happy home, one in which the whole family could flourish and grow.

A BBC television children's programme producer, John, had heard about our work and contacted us. He was interested in possibly doing a series of programmes focussing in turn on each country and Mark agreed to take him out to Belarus. He was enormously impressed and moved by the experience. On the last day after receiving warm hospitality from several of our families, we were late in arriving at the last home where we were due to have dinner. It was pitch dark when we arrived, but the family welcomed us with very generous glasses of vodka. Eventually the father said he would cook the meat on the barbecue. After a very short time he came back into the house with a plate full of charcoaled black joints of chicken. Mark put his knife into one bit and the blood spurted out so, wisely, he decided to leave the rest. John, however, who was very happy and relaxed after all the vodka, seemed not to notice and merrily ate all of his. It was a very jolly evening on which to end our visit. Early the following morning we flew back to the UK.

Returning home on a Belarussian aeroplane we were given a not very appetising tray of food which included a sachet of tomato ketchup. John had an important meeting on arrival in London so was wearing a very smart suit. Mark was having difficulty opening his sachet, when suddenly the ketchup spurted out all down John's shirt and tie. He was clearly not amused. Mark apologised profusely as John tried rather unsuccessfully to clean himself up. At the airport we parted on fairly good terms. However, we became concerned when we heard nothing from him. We thought the mishap might have diminished our chance of having some programmes made by him about our work. Two weeks later Mark telephoned him and a very weak voice said, *"Hello"*, to which Mark responded, *"John, it's Mark here. How are you?"* He replied, *"Well, I'm out of hospital now."* He was still recovering from a very bad dose of salmonella poisoning, obviously from the charcoaled chicken.

He did not pursue his idea of making programmes about our work, but he assured us that it had nothing to do with the chicken and ketchup disasters!

Galina

Whilst we had a good partnership with BCF, and respected all that they were doing for children in Belarus, it became clear that they did not agree that DI was essential. We therefore decided in 2006 to set up our own programme in the country and for this we needed someone special to run it. Bohdan had met Galina Schwarz, a Belarussian, in Minsk some years earlier, and he thought she would make an ideal Country Director. We invited her to

A loving family

the UK for an interview; her intelligence, perfect English and her compassion shone through and we were delighted to appoint her to the post.

At the time it was estimated that there were 159 children's institutions in the country, ten of which were baby homes. Immediately Galina set about closing the first institution in a town called Masti in the Grodno region. It was large, isolated and depressing. Luckily an enlightened Director and her helpful staff recognised that it was not the best place for 65 vulnerable children aged between 7 and 18. As we had found in other countries, the best advocates for DI are the Directors of the institutions who have witnessed the positive transformation in the lives of the children after they have been reintegrated with families. Galina oversaw the closure of two more institutions for children and she worked together with the Ministries of Health and Education to establish services to prevent the abandonment of children by desperate parents.

With a very small budget of about 1% of our annual expenditure, Galina and her small team have achieved great results. They have made good progress in advocating the need for reforming the childcare system in the country, demonstrating how it can be done and training people to carry it out.

ॐ

Bear watching the Sentsov family working on their home

VICTIMS OF RAPE
KOSOVO

SERBIA

MONTENEGRO

Mitrovice

Pristina

Peje

KOSOVO

Gjilan

Gjakove

Ferizaj

Prizren

ALBANIA

MACEDONIA

2001 - 2007

The Situation: A short brutal war in 1998 and 1999 resulted in thousands of people living in desperate poverty.

The Problem: Numerous abandoned babies and destitute children.

Our Initial Plan: To rescue 50 babies abandoned in the hospital in Pristina.

The Outcome: We created two homes and reintegrated all the babies into families before handing over the programme to a local NGO.

"Love is not consolation – it is light."
Anonymous

> *Inside we found 30 abandoned babies with their 'dead eyes open' - silently lying in rows of rusty cots. They were hidden away from the world. Their very existence was sensitive as most, if not all, were born as a result of rape. No-one wanted to know about them. Their future was bleak. They were destined for lives of misery and loneliness in a State orphanage devoid of any love or affection.*

The war in Kosovo between the Kosovo Liberation Army (mainly of Albanian origin) and the Serbian forces of the Republic of Yugoslavia was short - from February 1998 to June 1999 - but incredibly brutal. Many people were killed, numerous women raped, and thousands became refugees. An already poor country became poorer and, as always, it was the poverty-stricken people who suffered the most.

In 2000 we were told by one of our supporters, whose daughter had worked in the hospital in the capital, Pristina, that there were many abandoned babies there. As we were already working in neighbouring Albania we decided to fly up to Pristina to assess the situation. Much to our surprise, as well as that of others in Kosovo, we gained access to the hospital and were taken upstairs to a run-down, shabby ward in which the babies were being kept, hidden away. One of the 30 little children inside was Era. We were told she would probably never walk because she had spent so long in her cot.

Abandoned babies

On meeting the head of UNICEF in the country, we told her what we had found and discussed how we might be able to help. We agreed to establish a home in Pristina if we could find a suitable house. It would be our pilot project to begin rescuing the children. Our first challenge was to find the right house and a qualified person to run it.

Era with her new mummy

We were fortunate to meet a very positive and cheerful English nurse, Jacky Fleming. She was in Kosovo working with a team of international police officers who were helping the Kosovo police to counter child trafficking; this was a major problem at the time. Nearing the end of her contract and enthused by our wish to rescue the children, Jacky agreed to stay on and work for HHC. We found and bought a large detached house in Pristina which Jacky adapted, equipped and furnished for ten tiny children. A great networker, she was well-known in Pristina and soon recruited a local team of caring people. It included some British soldiers from the Black Watch who were stationed there at the time; they tackled the overgrown garden and built a play area.

The home Jacky created in Pristina had an especially happy and loving atmosphere. The first ten toddlers were brought from the hospital to the house in their drab clothing. They were pale, pathetic little ones, having never been outside the hospital ward since the day they were abandoned there. Within hours of their arrival in their colourful new home and dressed in their new clothes, they were showered with smiles and cuddles. A few weeks later the change in their behaviour was dramatic. They had become lovable little children. Finding families and foster parents for them in the state they were in when in hospital, would have been an impossible task. Now, everyone wanted to pick them up, hug them and take them home. And this is exactly what happened. Within the first 15 months 50 babies and toddlers had been found homes. Some of them were reunited with their natural families, others were adopted or fostered by local families. Era was fostered by a loving family, including a granny and an aunt, who obviously adored her. By her fifth birthday she was running around and playing with other children in her neighbourhood and helping a disabled man in her street with odd jobs, such as carrying his shopping. It was an amazing transformation – she was a happy little girl.

The house we bought in Pristina

At the beginning of 2002 we were asked to provide another home, this time in Prizren, the second largest town in Kosovo. It provided a sanctuary and a safe place for older vulnerable children in need of protection. We rented a large house with a garden in a quiet area on the outskirts of the town. Once more, Jacky created a warm, well-run and welcoming home. This was the only residential home for orphaned, abandoned or abused children in Kosovo, offering temporary care while they healed physically and psychologically and their future was planned. In the first year 24 children, mostly girls, were helped to reintegrate with their home communities. It was a remarkable achievement since all of the children had suffered in various appalling ways, including being raped and forced into prostitution.

Child trafficking was a terrible problem in the country. In 2003 we were asked by the Prime Minister's office to assist with the programme to combat this. At the same time we worked with vulnerable families to prevent their breakdown and we also contributed towards improving the foster care and adoption services in the country.

Karl Jenkins, the composer, who went out to visit our programme, with one of the familes

Clearly, people were recognising the value of our work in Kosovo. Even so, not everything was plain sailing. On one occasion we encountered the kind of corruption that can be very pervasive. The case involved one of

Children and staff in the home in Prizren

the local women we had employed to help in the office. She turned out to be incompetent and lazy; she spent more time smoking than working so we decided she must leave. Previously we had met her brother, a very suave man, who held a senior post in the Government. When he heard about his sister's dismissal he became extremely angry and abusive. He threatened us, saying that if his sister was not reinstated he would get our programme closed down and have us all thrown out of the country. We were shocked by his behaviour, but ignored his threats. Luckily for us nothing further happened.

After another year of doing invaluable work Jacky decided she needed a new challenge back in the UK. We had given many extremely vulnerable children the chance of a positive future. It seemed to us the right time to hand over our HHC programme to a new nationally registered NGO run by local people whom she had trained.

Skulls And Bones
Rwanda

2001 -

The Situation: Nearly one million people were killed in the four-month genocide in 1994. HIV / AIDS killed many more.

The Problem: An estimated 300,000 children were orphaned.

Our Initial Plan: To support some of the orphaned children.

The Outcome: We supported many vulnerable children and families. We continue to work with the Government to close their 34 orphanages.

"I give a lot of love to the children. I am wealthy in that and I give it freely."
Monique

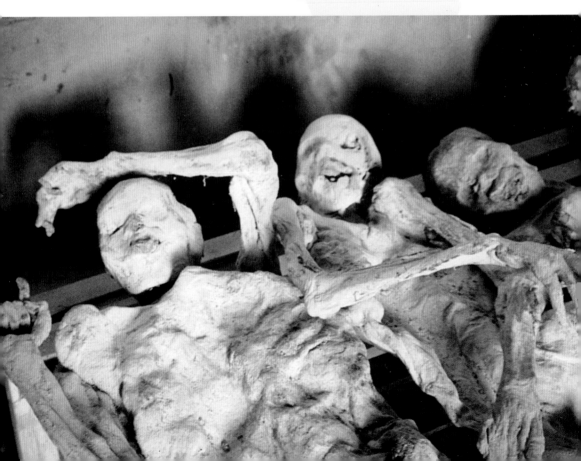

> *We were lucky that James had prepared us for what we were going to see – if indeed anything can prepare you for going into a little church where people sought refuge and had then been hacked to death. Their clothes were piled up in one corner and their bones in another; their skulls had been arranged like books on bookshelves around the walls, with the small baby skulls at the top and the large skulls lower down. Many of the skulls had been split by blows to the head from machetes. We saw many such places which exist today as 'shrines'; they are a reminder of what happened. Their message is stark ..."Never Again".*

In three months in 1994 nearly one million people were killed during the genocide in Rwanda, not by air strikes or artillery fire, but mostly by being hacked to death by machetes. The majority of the victims were Tutsis who had been killed by their Hutu neighbours, former friends and members of the local community. Thousands of children were bereft – with few if any family members still alive. And then HIV/AIDS struck and devastated already suffering families and whole communities. Life in refugee camps led to an increase in the number of HIV positive people resulting in even more children becoming orphans. Many of the widows who were raped during the genocide became HIV positive and subsequently died, leaving their children to look after themselves. Their situation was worse than desperate – it was disastrous; they had little or no hope for the future.

We were already working in four African countries, but being aware of the horrific genocide in Rwanda, we had, for a long time, wished to help the children there as well. In 2001 James Whiting heard about a Rwandan woman living in London who ran a charity called SURF (Survivors Fund) which raised money for Rwandan widows and he arranged to meet her. She told him how, after the war, a group of widows began to support one another. Hearing a distraught woman sobbing her heart out under a tree, a neighbour, passing by, stopped to console her. Soon a third widow joined them and then another and another – the group grew larger and larger. All of them were overcome with grief. These widows formed themselves into a very active organisation which they called Avega (Association des Veuves du Génocide – founded in 1995) with the specific aim *'to help widows and their dependents escape the poverty, anguish and misery that filled their lives following the 1994 genocide'.* We thought that Avega was just the sort of organisation we had been looking for, so James flew to Rwanda to meet its members. He met one of the widows, Monique, who was looking after 16 orphaned children. She told James, *"I cannot resist them. If they are orphans and come to me, I just say 'Yes'. Sometimes I wonder how can I feed all of them. They have a greater need of love than of material goods. I give a lot of love. I am wealthy in that and I give it freely."*

We will never forget James talking to us on the day he came back from his first visit. He was so moved and horrified by what he had seen and by the personal stories of the people he met. He had been totally unprepared for the whole shocking experience. One day he was taken by Avega women to a school which, they said, had been the site of a mass killing, but they did not tell him that the remains were still there. You can imagine his unbelievable horror when they opened the door into the first classroom where the bones of hundreds of bodies were laid out on racks. Just as shocking was hearing the testimonies of the widows, many of whom were the sole survivors of large families of 12 or more siblings. It made obvious sense to help these women look after their surviving children and support others who were orphaned and living without adult care. Within a few weeks we went out to meet them.

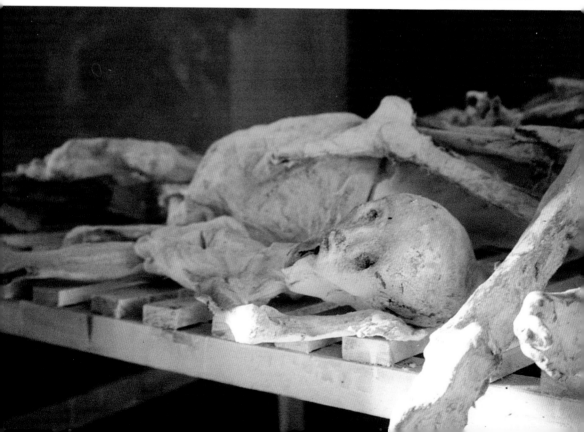

On our first day in Rwanda we met the Country Director of Save The Children. He was distraught. He had just been told by his Head Office to scale back the programme prior to a withdrawal, since the emergency was now over. More than 100 people were working with him. He said that the children needed support from them now more than ever, to help rebuild their lives. He was very pleased when we told him that this was exactly what we wanted to do. It was also a clear example for us of the difference between disaster relief operations and the type of recovery programme which required a long-term commitment. Some people assume that as soon as a war or disaster has ended, life can carry on as before, that the problem has gone away. Of course this is seldom the case. The aftermath of wars and disasters brings a different set of problems and often requires a complete rebuild of every aspect of the country and its infrastructure. In these situations it is incredibly difficult to know where to start and assess what the priorities are. It is inevitable that there will be insufficient funding to do everything at once. Very often the rebuilding of children's lives is very low down on the 'to do' list. And this is the time when our work can make a big impact.

Mike Milan, our Chairman of Trustees at the time, went on the next visit with Mark to meet Avega. It was agreed that the aims of our two organisations made it difficult for us to focus together on the people we both wanted to help. Their priority was widows, whereas ours was to support children, many of whom had no mother or grandmother. So in 2002 we decided that we should start HHC Rwanda. We were incredibly fortunate that Avega agreed to their Director of Programmes, Vianney Rangira, becoming our first Country Director. A quietly-spoken man, Vianney had the knowledge and experience and, most importantly, the passion, right from the start, for working with vulnerable children.

A very happy and special event happened on the last day of our visit. It was Vianney and Consolata's wedding day. Vianney invited us to be his guests at the celebration. Smartly dressed in his new suit, Vianney picked us up early in the morning and drove us to his bride's home in a village two hours' journey away. As is the custom, on our arrival we and all the other guests on the bridegroom's side of the family were made to wait outside. We were told that this could be for two hours or two days! By this time the sun was up and it was getting very hot. About 50 of us tried to get in the shade of the only tree on a bare piece of land nearby. Luckily, an hour later, we were invited into the garden of the house where an awning had been erected and two groups of plastic chairs had been arranged facing each other, one for the bride's family and friends and the other for the groom's. Between them there were two 'thrones' where eventually Consolata and Vianney came and sat, looking very serious and solemn. Then a dialogue between the two families started, trying to prove that their family was better than the other one and, therefore, the bride or the groom was not good enough. Stories were told about the other family and insults were thrown backwards and forwards, but it was all done in good humour. Presents were given including a cow, a plastic bucket, and a new garden hoe which was inspected very carefully to make sure that the quality of the metal was good. Unfortunately we had to leave the ceremony to go to the airport just as it was getting exciting.

Soon after our visit Vianney and a small team began working, initially with Avega. Cooperation with the widows was helpful in the early months. We supported over 400 children who were living in families headed either by a child or by a frail grandparent. According to their needs we gave them food, repaired their houses, helped develop farming projects and some micro-enterprise schemes; we also gave them any necessary training and where possible enabled them to go to school. Our aim was to keep the siblings together, giving all the children the chance to look after one another within their own family. This was an important but very difficult task when neither parent was alive to care for them.

Making friends with a little girl minding goats

Our HHC Rwanda team worked hard and grew in number. Ideas began to develop and one of these proved to be very beneficial for the children. Very often these child-headed households were in small, remote villages and the children were very vulnerable to all manner of dangers. Often they were scared and had no-one to turn to for help or advice. We met one girl, about 12 years old, looking after three younger siblings in their family home. They had two small goats which they brought into their tiny house every night afraid that they would be stolen if they left them tethered outside. We felt desperately sorry for these and other children like them who felt alone and isolated. Their lives were full of constant fear.

Realising we had to do something to help them, our Rwandan team came up with a great idea. Rather than approaching an adult in the village and asking them to keep an eye on the children our staff asked the children themselves who they liked and trusted. Very often that person was not the most obvious

Sharing time with a child-headed family

one in the community. Our team then met the person, and explained that the children themselves had chosen them to be their mentors. Almost on every occasion the person was very pleased and willing to take on the role – it gave them a sense of worth and of being wanted. Within a short time 60 people had been chosen and were called Wise Persons. From then on, whenever one of our staff members went to check on the children, they would go and speak to the Wise Person too, to find out if there were any problems. Dorothea, one of these, said, *"I am truly honoured to be chosen as a Wise Person. It is so important to support our vulnerable children and help them realise that there is someone who cares for them and that they do have a future."*

We were particularly concerned for the safety of some of the extremely vulnerable granny- and child-headed households who lived in very isolated areas. We created a small 'village' of 15 small houses for them a few miles from Kigali so that they had the extra security of living close to one another.

Happy children unaware of the horrors of the past

A purpose-built centre was at the heart of the community; it consisted of four separate rooms and a kitchen. In the day time, whilst the youngest children attended the nursery school, their mothers engaged in various other activities, including parenting skills. An important element of the programme was the preparation of nutritional food for the children. Other members of the wider community made good use of this facility. It became our first Community Hub and the model for similar Hubs in Rwanda and eventually in other countries. We went out with Clare de Lore and Audrey Paisey for the opening of the homes and Centre; this was a very jolly occasion with lots of singing and dancing.

Whilst there we went to see a widower who was dying of AIDS. A tall gaunt man, he was surprised when we arrived. He lived in a tiny grass house with his two small sons, aged about five and six. The only pieces of furniture in their home were a few wooden stools, a bench and a table on which was a large book – we presumed it was a bible. We sat and talked with him. All the time he had his arms around his two young boys who sat next to him on the bench and kept looking up at him. You could feel the love father and sons shared together, but we all knew the father's life would end soon. His only concern was for his children and what was going to happen to them. He had just one surviving relative, a widowed sister who lived a long way away and was overwhelmed with the problems of looking after too many children herself. We promised him that we would care for his sons. We could see that he felt a great sense of relief that, at last, someone was going to relieve him of his biggest anxiety.

Before we left Mark asked him if the book was a bible and he said, "Yes." We asked him if he would read a passage and he agreed. We handed it to him and still sitting with his sons, he read a passage at random in Kinyarwanda, which of course, we could not understand. Our interpreter said it was about a stranger helping a sick person. For us it was a painfully moving experience. As we left the family, the father showed us where they slept on the floor, covered by a few dirty old blankets. He said when it was cold at night, they slept very close together to keep one another warm. But he knew that he would not be there to do this for much longer.

We were very fortunate that Don McKinnon, the Commonwealth Secretary General, agreed to become one of our Patrons shortly after he took up his appointment in 2001. He, and his wife Clare de Lore, who twice visited Rwanda with us, became very active and enormously helpful supporters of HHC, hosting events at their home and in Marlborough House in London, the headquarters of the Commonwealth. They also opened many doors for us to people with influence – one of them being President Kagame of Rwanda.

In November 2007 we hosted a conference in Kigali to showcase our model of family support which had already enabled us to transform the lives of about 140 families. As President Kagame was very keen for Rwanda to become a

Vianney on his wedding day

member of the Commonwealth he agreed to meet us and attend the conference. Before the start we (Mark with Clare de Lore, Delia and Joe Glackin) met with the President for half an hour and told him about our experience in Rwanda and other countries, and our wish to work with his Government to reform their childcare system. As the President was attending the conference, his Prime Minister and most of the Cabinet were also present. This gave us a wonderful opportunity to get our message across.

The real star of the conference was a 19 year old boy, Jean-Marie. He had a young brother and sister whom he had been doing his best to look after following the death of their parents. He explained that he had asked many organisations to help him but none had, and then he heard about HHC. He went to the office and met Vianney and his team who all listened to him. It was, he said, the first time anyone had really listened to his story. They discussed ideas for his future including giving him a skill so that he could become self-sufficient and look after his siblings. Vianney suggested various options – engineering, building or tailoring. He chose tailoring and an apprenticeship with a tailor was organised for him. Jean-Marie learned quickly. We gave him micro-credit to buy a sewing machine and in no time at all he started his own business. Very soon he had earned enough money to buy a cow to provide milk for his family, and he sold any that was surplus. As he finished telling his story everyone clapped. There was a pause and then he said, *"Actually I am a very good tailor as you can see by the suit I'm wearing. Many people come to me, especially for wedding clothes and I have now got two cows!"* At this point everyone clapped again, even louder than before. Roars of laughter filled the hall. Jean-Marie was a wonderful example of how just the right amount of support can transform the lives of a destitute family and enable them to become self-sufficient and independent.

At the lunch we had organised to follow the conference Mark sat next to a Senator, whose name was Odette. She told him that she was the only one of 14 siblings who had survived the genocide. During the conversation she mentioned orphanages and until that moment we had not realised that there were any in Rwanda. She agreed to

Jean-Marie with his first cow

Delia

take Mark and Delia to one in Kigali after lunch. It was called the Home of Hope run by an order of nuns. Home of Hope was a total misnomer! There were dozens of silent babies and small children in cots - so close together that it was difficult to walk between them - and it was stiflingly hot. Down a slope there was another long building where older children and adults were lying in their beds in a comatose state, as if sedated. We asked what happened to the younger children and we were told that many were sent abroad for adoption. Those who weren't adopted would probably finish up going down the slope to join the older ones. We were very distressed to hear of this practice. (We are now in the process of closing this orphanage.)

After this experience we discovered that there were 34 orphanages in Rwanda. In 2010 the Government asked for our support and technical assistance in closing all of them down. Vianney, who had worked tirelessly for us for nearly ten years, became our Regional Childcare Adviser and we were extremely fortunate in appointing Claudine Nyinawagaga as Country Director as his successor. She had previously been the Mayor of Gasabo, the biggest district in Kigali.

Rick Foulsham in the first Community Hub in Rwanda

A boy with his 'bicycle taxi' purchased with micro-credit funding

A boy with his wooden bike, called a 'igitogotogo', to carry goods for people

Our Patron Nick Hewer, with a teenager who set up an egg business using micro-credit funding

A 72 year old blind grandmother looking after four grandchildren whose parents were killed in the genocide

(from left) Annonciata, Manager of the Mpore Pefa orphanage which we closed, with Mary Wakefield, Vianney, Epa, a staff member of HHC Rwanda and Victoria Martin, our Senior Programmes Manager

In 2011 Mary Wakefield, Deputy Editor of *The Spectator*, visited our programme in Rwanda. In the magazine on 6 October she wrote, '*It was heartbreaking to see children either totally ignored or clamouring to be hugged. But it was wonderful to know that the HHC team were on the case like detectives, tracking down the children's families and finding them homes. Before my visit I had no idea that most institutionalised children were not actually 'orphans' and had parents or grandparents. I now understand the immense difference between an institution and a family. The reintegrated children I met looked proud; they suddenly belonged. Hope and Homes for Children has really given me new faith in charities.*'

Today we have become the Rwandan Government's main partner in developing more effective childcare systems across the country. Together we are developing a national family-based care system for orphaned and vulnerable children and we are aiming to close the remaining 33 institutions, making Rwanda the first country in Africa to be free from institutional care for children. So far we have closed one institution and are currently closing two more, one of which contains over 550 children and young adults. Following on from Vianney's pioneering work in laying a firm foundation for us in Rwanda, our programme is now having an increasing impact in the country under the inspiring leadership of Claudine. It is now our leading model of DI in Africa.

༄

THE SILENT KILLER
SOUTH AFRICA

2001 - 2013

The Situation: 8,000 people were dying of HIV / AIDS every day.

The Problem: Countless children lost one or both parents.

Our Initial Plan: To help orphaned siblings, often in child-headed households, to stay together in their own homes.

The Outcome: Numerous families were helped. We handed over our programmes to other NGOs.

"Let us not equivocate: a tragedy of unprecedented proportion is unfolding in Africa. AIDS today in Africa is claiming more lives than the sum of all wars, famines and floods, and the ravages of such deadly diseases as malaria …. Children's lives are on the line and this time the enemy is AIDS."

Nelson Mandela

As we entered the hut we could make out in the light of a flickering candle the face of a little girl and an aged grandmother. On a mattress on the floor lay the motionless body of the child's mother, barely able to move her eyes to see us. She had AIDS and only about two days to live. The granny asked us to join hands and she offered up a heartfelt beseeching prayer for her daughter. As we left, the child was sitting on the bed staring blankly at her mother. (James Whiting)

We decided that we had to do something to help orphans of AIDS in South Africa. Our declared mission at the time was … *To provide homes for orphans of war or disaster* and there was no bigger disaster than AIDS. It was estimated by the AIDS Foundation of South Africa that 8,000 people were dying of HIV / AIDS related diseases every day in the country and that there would eventually be over one million orphans of AIDS; one out of every three children would have no parents.

Whereas the usual images of famine, conflict and natural disasters rouse the emotions and result in huge responses to appeals, this does not happen in the case of AIDS. AIDS kills silently and the pain and grief are borne by families in thousands of homes across Africa. This has made fundraising for AIDS difficult – and indeed some of our supporters thought that we should not get involved in helping children in Africa because of the fear that the money might be wasted. This attitude made us even more determined that we should do something, however small our contribution.

As James Whiting had spent a year working in South Africa we asked him to go out there in 2001 to assess what, if anything, we could do to help at least some of these desperate children. He found four highly-committed local organisations in the poorest, most deeply affected parts of the country and we decided to support the work they were doing. The families were usually headed by children or grandparents and all were affected and made particularly vulnerable by HIV / AIDS and poverty. We discovered that many of them were illiterate and living in remote rural areas. Very often the children had not been registered at birth and the social workers spent an enormous amount of time in Government offices trying to prove their existence. This was essential in order that support from the Government's social security system could be obtained.

James with 'the boys'

In 2003 we went to see the situation for ourselves and were deeply moved by some of the families we met and the stories we heard. One little girl, aged about 7 years old, had nursed her dying mother, trying to give her food and keep her clean; she had very little outside assistance. One night she realised that she desperately needed help as her mother's condition had worsened, so she put her in a wheel barrow and pushed her almost five kilometres to the nearest clinic ... where she died. We met the little girl shortly afterwards, confused and alone in her house. We were told that other family members were trying to lay claim to the house which was the young girl's rightful inheritance and her only guarantee for a hopeful future. Such stories, we were told, were common.

One of our projects was in the black township of Umtata which is where James had worked in a school years before. On our arrival we met Sister Mary Paule, the staff and numerous small children, including the many tiny babies they were looking after. We had arranged to stay there in the convent for the night and it was a particular pleasure to spend some time with Sister Mary Paule. James had told us so much about his respect and admiration for her as a person and the amazing work she had been doing in South Africa for many years. She told us that of all the volunteers who had helped in

James with a grandfather, caring alone for his grandchildren

the school over the years James stood out as being particularly special. Later that day we were told about three teenagers who were living on their own in a house on a hill just outside Umtata. With some difficulty we found the house just as it was beginning to get cold and dark. Arriving unexpectedly, the three young people were very surprised to see us and obviously embarrassed. The house had a bedroom, sitting room and an outside kitchen. It was very clean and tidy and it seemed to us that the three teenagers had been sitting and talking together when we appeared.

The oldest boy was about 17 with a younger sister and brother; they had obviously been well cared for in the past. They explained that their parents had died a year earlier and they had no money left to buy school uniforms and shoes, so they could no longer go to school. They showed us their old school clothes, still on hangers in a cupboard, and shoes that were far too small. They also proudly got out their old school books and showed us the good marks they had received. The outside kitchen was empty – there was not a single morsel of food anywhere. We asked them what they were going to eat that night and they said they would drink water. Even that was a problem as they had to collect the drinking water from a factory two kilometres away since the local supply was contaminated.

Their situation was desperate and was about to become worse. The sister was obviously about eight months pregnant. Clearly she had been the breadwinner; but now, not only was there no bread, there was about to be another mouth to feed. We imagined the conversation they were having when we arrived - the sister telling her brothers that she had *'done her bit'* and the boys arguing about how they were going to get food. They were being forced by circumstances completely beyond their control to take some sort of drastic action, just to survive. Overcome by the hopelessness of their situation Caroline said, *"We must find some food for them now, this evening, enough to last them a few days until our team in Umtata can make plans for their future."* So, we took the oldest boy in our vehicle to the nearest store, about five miles away where, with our encouragement, he chose food for the next few days. We were very touched that he obviously felt embarrassed to be spending so much of our money. As we drove away from their house we wondered how many more young people there were like these throughout Africa, suffering in a similar way that very night.

We were fortunate that two very good supporters, Brigadier Gordon Hughes and his wife Liz, were living in Johannesburg at the time; Gordon was Commander of the British Army Training Team there. They had made friends with an extraordinarily positive and compassionate woman, Mpho, and were supporting the hospice she had started in a town called Moreteli, about one and a half hours' drive from Johannesburg. We stayed with Gordon and Liz and went to meet Mpho. She took us to see some of the families she and her team were helping. In each home there was a member, normally the mother or father, dying of AIDS, leaving children behind, often completely on their own. Mpho's team were working with the whole family through this distressing, painful and messy process, and preparing and planning the children's future. In one house we visited there were two teenage girls living alone. They were so ashamed that their parents had died of AIDS and so afraid of their own vulnerability that they, too, had stopped going to school. They rarely went outside and kept their door locked at all times. We were deeply moved by all we had witnessed. Inspired by Mpho we decided we should start supporting the organisation she had created called *'The Moretele Sunrise Hospice'*.

Following our visit to the various programmes in South Africa we went to see Caroline's brother, Martin, on his farm in the Northern Transvaal and spent a very happy few days with him. He was the third generation of his family to farm there. Very sadly it was the last time we saw him. Not long afterwards he was shot and killed one night at the gate of his farm. He was discovered the next morning with his loyal Jack Russell dog, Wups, standing beside him. Martin was just one of over 1,000 white farmers murdered in South Africa including a number of his friends.

Immediately we heard the terrible news we flew out to South Africa to organise Martin's funeral, as he was not married. William came with us and Edward joined us from Australia. A week later, Edward left and unfortunately we also had to return home because of our HHC commitments. Luckily William was able to stay behind to sort everything out, but we were extremely anxious knowing that he was alone on the farm on which his uncle had just been killed.

Initially we managed our partnerships with the four organisations from the UK, but we wanted to expand our work in the KwaZulu-Natal area and needed a strong and experienced local manager. We were lucky to find Sister Silke Malmain who was working in the country at the time. Sister Silke was a young German nun with a great sense of humour; and she had a very pragmatic opinion on the AIDS pandemic and how to prevent it spreading further.

We appointed Sister Silke as our Country Representative in January 2004. She very quickly established a good working relationship between the staff in the projects and HHC staff in the UK. She became a wonderful ambassador for our work, talking at various high-profile events in the UK

Sister Silke carrying a Bible in one hand and cans of beer in the other

Sister Silke taking Claire Lanham, (a member of our HHC staff) and two of our Patrons, Claire Wright (second left) and Rotarian Gordon McInally, to meet families in KwaZulu-Natal. Gordon was RIBI President, and he and his whole family have been great supporters

and was very popular with everyone – particularly Rotarians. We all loved her!

Unfortunately at the end of 2005 she was posted by her Order to Mozambique. Our programmes continued and expanded in South Africa, overseen by Joe Glackin who was appointed our Regional Manager for Africa and then subsequently our Head of Strategic Development. Joe had worked in Africa for many years in Liberia and Sudan. His experience, charm and great sense of humour were exactly what we needed.

Joe Glackin in action

In 2013 we handed over our current programmes to local authorities whilst our future possible involvement in South Africa is being reassessed.

∽

We heard the unbelievably shocking news in June 2014 that Sister Mary Paule had also been murdered. She was 82 and had been doing wonderful work in South Africa for nearly 60 years.

∽

CAGED IN
TRANSNISTRIA

2000 -

The Situation: This small region broke away from Moldova in a short war in 1991-92 and aligned itself with Russia.

The Problem: Desperate poverty led to the abandonment of children into orphanages.

Our Initial Plan: To rescue one girl being kept in a cage.

The Outcome: Rescued 60 girls from an orphanage and we are engaged in closing another institution.

"There is always one moment in childhood when the door opens and lets the future in."
Graham Greene

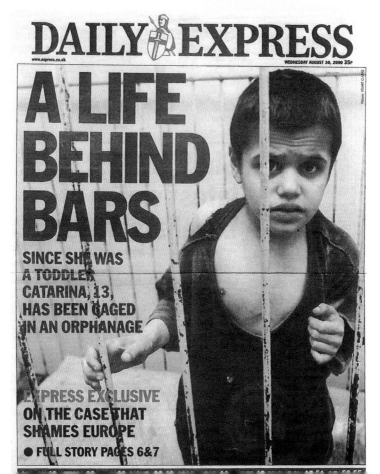

There were numerous women with mental disabilities shuffling around the grounds and 45 girls, mostly teenagers with various disabilities, were being kept in one small building nearby. Mingling daily with the older women obviously exacerbated the girls' own problems. Their living conditions were appalling; they included an 'activities room' which was small and dark. The stench hit us before our eyes got adjusted to the darkness. The room was crowded with teenage girls with special needs, some of them up against the walls, others crouching on the floor in a foetal position and covered in their own excrement. Amongst them was Catarina. Yet again we were confronted with a horrific nightmare situation. We had to rescue her and all the other children from this hellhole, as soon as possible.

We will never forget Tuesday 29 August 2000. Caroline received yet another totally unexpected telephone call which was, ultimately, to change the lives of hundreds of children. The call was from a journalist at the *Daily Express* newspaper who told her that one of their freelance reporters had discovered a girl being kept in a cage in Transnistria and that the paper was going to run the story the next day. He asked Caroline if HHC would be prepared to try and get the girl out if details about our charity were printed at the bottom of the article. He said it would give us useful publicity. He wanted a straight 'yes or no' reply within the hour! At the time Mark was in Ukraine with Bohdan and a potential major donor, driving along a remote road on their way to visit one of our homes. Mark's mobile phone suddenly rang, but the reception was so poor he had to stop the car, get out and stand on the roadside. With difficulty he just managed to hear Caroline's voice. An instant decision had to be made. After a brief discussion with Bohdan who knew the breakaway region well, Mark and Caroline decided to accept this totally new challenge. Another 'interesting' adventure was about to begin!

The following day a photograph of the girl, Catarina, filled the whole of the front page of the newspaper. It was absolutely shocking. It touched the hearts of many *Daily Express* readers who immediately pledged money for Catarina's release.

The first question was how to get into Transnistria? We were advised that the best way was through Moldova. Fortunately Bohdan was able to find a useful contact for us – a Moldovan woman who was willing to arrange our visit. Shortly afterwards we flew out together with our young PA, Becky Shaw. The woman met us at Chisinau airport and told us that Moldova was an extremely dangerous place for foreigners and that we might be mugged if we stayed in an hotel. 'For our safety' she had arranged for us to stay 'at a reasonable rate' in a flat belonging to one of her friends who was not using it that week. She drove us to a very run-down back street and stopped outside a drab, dilapidated block of flats. Our hearts sank. She escorted us up the dirty concrete steps to the fifth floor and into the apartment. It was clear that the owner – who was probably the woman herself – had left in a hurry leaving many personal things behind including a toothbrush and toothpaste. Was this a way for her to make some money? The flat was quite disgusting and sordid, but not knowing what else we could do, we had to stay for the two nights. Poor Becky was horrified and found it so awful that she chose to sleep in a chair rather than in an unclean bed!

The next morning the woman collected us and we drove to the Transnistrian border. It was manned by Russian police and soldiers with old tanks and gun positions in sandbag bunkers. The whole atmosphere was tense, hostile and intimidating. Grim-faced men grunted instructions at us and pointed to a hut. In this 'office' our passport details were laboriously written down. Finally, over an hour later, we were given our visas … for a three-hour visit!

Catarina was being kept in an orphanage in a town called Bender, about 20 miles from the border. We drove as quickly as we could and arrived at a large foreboding-looking complex of concrete buildings with huge metal gates controlled by a guard. We sensed immediately that we were not welcome. The guard had a long phone call with someone. Eventually we were escorted into a building and taken to the Director's office. The Director was a man in his 50s or 60s; clearly he was not happy to see us. When we told him we would like to see Catarina he immediately made a telephone call to somebody else. He started to sweat and shake with fear as the person on the other end of the line was shouting angrily, obviously giving him strict instructions that on no account was he to let us in to see anyone. News of the *Daily Express* article and photograph had obviously reached the ears of officials in Transnistria and they were not pleased – hence our very hostile reception. We were extremely disappointed that we were prevented from meeting Catarina and the other girls. From what we saw and heard we deduced that the place was, in fact, a women's mental asylum and totally unsuitable for children of any age.

We were back at the border within three hours and on returning to Chisinau we went directly to the UNICEF office to find out more about the situation in Moldova and Transnistria. We discussed different ideas with a very helpful Italian woman who was the head of the UNICEF mission in both countries. We had made a commitment to ensure that Catarina was released and knew that we would have to return to Bender as soon as possible. If we did not, how else could we be certain that she was out of the cage? And what about the plight of the other girls in that appalling place?

Over the next few weeks lengthy discussions and negotiations took place with UNICEF in Moldova and, through them, the authorities in Transnistria. It was imperative to move the girls out of the asylum as quickly as possible and we agreed to work together to achieve this. The local authority in Bender offered us a disused school which, they suggested, could become a suitable place to accommodate the girls. Like so many buildings we saw, it was run-down and dilapidated but over the following year, we refurbished it, creating a home-like environment and a much-needed Rehabilitation Centre. Soon afterwards we bought three small houses to provide homes for the girls with severe physical and mental disabilities. While this was going on Georgette and other childcare specialists and volunteers, including Kerry, carried out a detailed assessment of each girl and prepared an individual care plan for them. It was an incredibly difficult and miserable environment in which to work. At one stage there was severe political unrest which made life even more dangerous for our HHC team, but they valiantly carried on the vital work in spite of it.

Finally we succeeded in moving all the girls out of the adult mental institution. Some were reintegrated with their families, others moved to the Centre, while those who had severe disabilities went into the three small homes. This programme was one of the most challenging we had ever experienced due to the politically unstable environment. Within months of their release from the asylum the transformation in the behaviour of many of the girls was remarkable.

Left to right: Elena, Liliana Rotaru, and a lady from the local authority in the ktchen of the new house

Elena on right, with her small team

Elena Karaivanova

It soon became apparent that one of the houses was too small, but fortunately the local authority offered us a plot of land nearby on which to build a specially designed home. Disappointingly this all took far longer than we would have liked due to numerous bureaucratic complications, but eventually a beautiful house, funded by one of our very generous supporters, was built. Mark went out to see it in March 2014 and was very impressed with the appropriate design for disabled children and young people and the quality of the building. Mrs Elena Karaivanova, the Head of our partner organisation in Transnistria, Hope for Families and Children (HFC), personally supervised the interior décor creating an attractive and colourful home for 12 girls with special needs.

On the same visit Mark was pleased to see that the Centre was being well-run and maintained. The girls were all busily engaged in various practical activities when he arrived and there was a great buzz and much laughter. They now have a quality of life which is far removed from the conditions in which we found them 14 years ago.

The new house

In 2013, with the help of other experts in childcare, we conducted an assessment of the childcare system in Transnistria. It highlighted the great need for reform in the country and clearly indicated a unique and extraordinary challenge for the future. Currently the small team of five people in HFC is working with the local authority in closing a baby orphanage in Tiraspol. The team members are also promoting new services such as a Mother and Baby Centre and a Day Care Centre for disabled children, as well as supporting vulnerable families in their homes.

Sadly Catarina died a few years after she moved into her new home, but we hope that while she was there she felt the healing power of love. It is highly unlikely that we would ever have started working in Transnistria or Moldova had Caroline not received that telephone call from the *Daily Express*. It is extraordinary to think that Catarina's suffering led us on a path which is continuing to change the lives of many children in Moldova and Transnistria.

ॐ

NIGHTMARE INSTITUTIONS
MOLDOVA

2001 -

The Situation: A former Communist regime, it is one of the poorest countries in Europe which had a short war in 1991-92 with its breakaway region Transnistria.

The Problem: Desperate poverty led to abandonment of children into institutions.

Our Initial Plan: To help the existing small family-type homes which were in dire need of support and to create more homes for vulnerable children.

The Outcome: We developed 53 homes and are now engaged in closing institutions.

"There is never any closure for the extreme pain that is heaped upon children such as myself, one of the unlucky ones. But there is a light in the world … it is made from pure love and you can live in it. It will give you strength, hope, courage, belief and one day you will find that you can actually shine it on others. If you get the chance to do so, don't let it pass you by."

Paolo Hewitt

Situated in a remote location outside Urhay, a village one hour's drive south of Chisinau, was a 'home' for 321 boys and young men with special needs. They all slept in metal cots lined up in rows and segregated according to their disability. The building was poorly insulated. In the winter it was as bitterly cold inside as it was outside. The children suffered badly as they were physically unable to walk around to keep warm. Worst of all they were starved of attention and affection with only one care worker looking after 25 disabled children.

Following our commitment in Transnistria and having already made contacts in Moldova, in 2001 we asked Bohdan to investigate if there was a need for our work and, if so, what the possibility was of starting a project there. He discovered that there were already 29 family-type homes in the country, similar to the ones we had established in Ukraine and we decided that we should undertake a survey of all of these to find out more. We were shocked by what Bohdan discovered. The support that the families were receiving from the State had not increased over many years and some benefits had not been paid at all. Houses were crumbling, food was in short supply and the dedicated 'parent/educators', who shared their family homes with a small number of 'orphans', were desperate. These families and all the children were becoming increasingly vulnerable and in danger of breaking down.

In January 2002 Mark went to Moldova with Bohdan and had a meeting with the President which was reported at length on television. We shared our findings with him and as a result a conference to highlight the plight of these forgotten families was arranged. Eventually money was found by the authorities to upgrade the houses and triple the living allowance of the families. At very little cost to HHC we had managed to avert another tragedy for the children by alerting the Government to the situation. As a result of the increase in family allowance 40 more children were taken in to these homes. We continued to monitor the progress of these families whilst creating three new homes.

As Bohdan was already overseeing our work in Ukraine and Belarus, we needed an office and somebody to be responsible for our work in Moldova and Transnistria. Bohdan found a Moldovan woman who seemed to have

A happy foster mother with one of her sons

all the right qualities and contacts in both countries. In the early stages she proved to be very useful, opening doors which gave us access to Government Ministers.

Over the following five years we were instrumental in developing a network of 53 homes across the whole of Moldova which saved 500 or more children from a miserable existence in State institutions. But we were acutely aware that this was not going to stop more children being placed in them and we began talks with Government officials and other agencies about reforming their institutionalised care system for children. It was estimated that there

Liliana Rotaru

were over 8,000 children at the time in 67 institutions regulated by three different Ministries. 98% of the children had parents. The extreme poverty in the country had resulted in the break-up of numerous families often leading to placing children in institutions.

During this time Bohdan had met the dynamic Liliana Rotaru, who had started a Moldovan childcare charity, Copil Comunitate Familia

(CCF) and was highly respected for the work she and her team were doing. Their commitment to reforming the childcare system dovetailed with our own mission so well that, having discussed it with Liliana, we decided to form a partnership and close down our office in Chisinau.

In 2008 we signed an agreement with the Ministry of Social Protection, Family and Child, to give them technical assistance in carrying out the first closure of an institution in Moldova at Urhay. This is a very complex project because of the range of special needs of all these vulnerable young people and is still not completed.

The following year we were given the go-ahead to start closing the second institution at Cupcui in Leova County, south west of Chisinau; 59 children lived there. An integral element of closing this institution was working with the local authorities to develop services that supported families at risk and enabled all of the children to be reintegrated with their communities. Without this range of services being firmly established the closure could not take place.

We have always been particularly concerned about abandoned babies and increasingly our priority has become the closure of baby homes. It is essential for their all round

Kate Adie

development that babies and very young children grow up within a loving family. Babies' brains grow at a phenomenal rate in the first two years of life. Without receiving individual affection and stimulation the brain's growth is stunted. This can lead to irreversible physical, cognitive and psychological damage which is likely to affect a child for the rest of their life.

For this reason we decided in 2010 that the next institution that we had to close should be the Municipal Institution for Babies in Chisinau. By carrying out these three closures, each a different type, it demonstrated that it was possible to reform all areas of Moldova's childcare system so that eventually every child could have the chance to fulfil their potential.

Kate Adie, one of our Patrons, went to Moldova in early 2010 with Mark and James Ruddy to see our work in the country. During her trip, Kate went to several institutions and met a number of the families we had supported. On her return she presented our Radio 4 Appeal to highlight awareness of our work as well as raise vital funds. She said *"In Moldova recently I came out of a freezing, barrack-like building which had lately housed dozens of neglected children and met local officials who had finally been convinced by the charity that there are better ways of caring for children. I met several families who had been given practical help and got to know their own children again. I saw the bright eyes and continuing surprise in the faces of children cared for by kind and enthusiastic foster parents – a life of warmth and love, away from the nightmare of the institutions."*

By 2012, a total of 18 institutions for children had been closed. The Government has made a commitment to continue the programme of reform and ensure a family environment for all children by closing all the remaining institutions.

Our work in Moldova, in partnership with Liliana and her tireless professional team, continues to go from strength to strength. In 2009 CCF was given a prestigious Human Rights Award for their work. On receiving it Liliana said, *"This is a momentous day for 8,000 children growing up in institutions in Moldova. It marks the beginning of the end of institutions. Let us hope that our achievements inspire a truly national effort with unstoppable momentum."*

❧

Our Patron, Kate Adie, visiting one of the families (opposite)

SAVING BABIES FIRST
BULGARIA

2009 -

The Situation: The country was admitted to the EU in 2007 after years of Communist rule which resulted in widespread poverty.

The Problem: Over 8,000 children existed in State institutions.

Our Initial Plan: To close one institution for babies 0-3 years.

The Outcome: The institution was closed. Work continues to close others and reform the whole childcare system.

"We are proving the true meaning of our common humanity.
To be human means to love."
Arki Busson

> *A baby, only a month old, was institutionalised totally against the will of his mother. Their doctor had recommended to the local Child Protection Department that the child, who has cerebral palsy, be placed in an institution because the mother would not be able to care for him. She said in horror, "I am trapped. I cannot do anything to keep my child!" After we got involved, our specialist consultant concluded that the child needed treatment for his fits, but that he could be cared for at home by the mother. We arranged this and supported them to attend a neurological clinic in Sofia. In addition, we uncovered that the hospital had been colluding with a baby institution to make misleading or exaggerated diagnoses and 'provide' children to keep the institution population high and ensure their Government budget is protected. (Galya Pourcheva-Bisset)*

Not long after we started HHC we had been encouraged by a member of another children's charity to think about starting a programme in Bulgaria. We were told that there was a great need for our work there – and that Bulgarian wine was excellent! Although the thought of the wine was a great attraction, we decided that we really did not have sufficient resources to do anything in the country, but we always kept in mind that one day we would like to do so. At a later date, following our partnership with ARK in Romania, Arki Busson, the Chairman, also tried to persuade us to work in Bulgaria, with their support, but once again we lacked the capacity to start a completely new programme.

Galya Pourcheva-Bisset

In the autumn of 2009 there was a change of Government in the country. Having heard of our work in neighbouring Romania, the new Government welcomed our interest in helping them to close their institutions and tackle the problem of child abandonment. There were over 8,000 children in State institutions and our priority, as always, was to rescue the babies (0–3 years) first, to minimise the damage that institutional care causes to children.

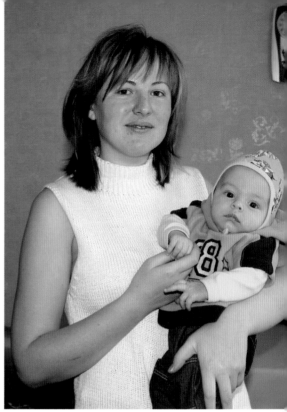

Rick with a picture made out of buttons given to him by a little girl who had been in an orphanage

A mother reunited with her son

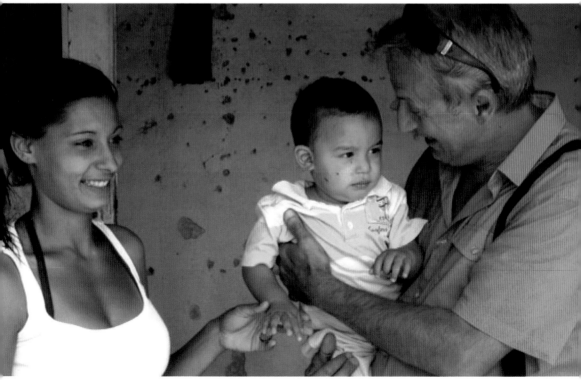

Georgi Simeonov known as Joro

We had appointed Galya Pourcheva-Bisset, a Bulgarian, as our Regional Coordinator in Central and Eastern Europe in 2007. She lives in Bulgaria with her Scottish husband and their children and speaks fluent English. Her wide experience of working in the child protection field and her extensive range of contacts made starting a new project in her country a natural decision.

Galya, who told us the sad story of the mother and her baby who had cerebral palsy, commented that this kind of corruption is all too common in some of the countries in which we are working. Her statement supports our own observation. As a result, families are being torn apart. Working in these circumstances, seemingly against all the odds, only increases our resilience and determination to overcome all the difficulties.

Rick Foulsham, HHC's CEO at the time, went to Bulgaria to discuss plans with the Government. It was agreed that the first baby institution to be closed should be the Teteven Institution for Babies (0–3 years). Working with Equilibrium, a local NGO, the institution was closed in 2010 and all the babies were reunited with their families. The building itself was converted into a Centre for Social Support providing a range of services for children and families. This was a great achievement and its success is due to the tenacity and sustained commitment of Georgi Simeonov, our Country Director, and his small team, supported most ably by Galya.

Following the success of the Teteven closure, the Government asked for our help to close a further eight baby institutions in the country as part of their National Strategy to reform their childcare system over the next 15 years.

There is much more to do in Bulgaria - and in so many other countries around the world.

༈

DEVELOPMENT AND SUCCESSION

Having decided to start the charity, Mark commuted some of his Army pension to get us going. Initially we worked at home and after a few months we moved to the top floor of a barn, just five minutes away. We employed a secretary, and a volunteer book-keeper who came in several evenings a week and kept an eye on our accounts. In the early years we went out to every new country together; it was essential that we both agreed the plan of action and could speak with one voice and with knowledge, conviction and passion. This was vitally important for our credibility. As we became increasingly busy it was necessary for one of us, normally Caroline, to be in the office whilst the other one, usually Mark, went out fundraising in this country and visiting our projects overseas.

We were lucky to get considerable media coverage from television and radio stations, as well as from newspapers and magazines. Donations followed. We were so surprised and humbled that people trusted us, that we felt we wanted to thank everyone personally and as quickly as possible. Over the years we have sent out thousands of handwritten letters and made countless telephone calls to people who have kindly sent us money. We felt strongly that we had two important moral responsibilities – first and foremost to the children, to do what was best in their long-term interests, and secondly, to our supporters to use their donations wisely and correctly for the children's future. We became a bridge linking our generous donors with the vulnerable children.

From the start, our major passion and priority has always been the children and how we can change their lives. Fundraising, which consumed most of our time, was the 'means to the end'. We just did not have extra time, interest or capacity to devote to all the other aspects needed to run a fast-expanding 'business', employing numerous people at home and abroad. Staff appraisals, health and safety procedures, risk assessments and detailed business plans were, for us, not priorities. It was obvious why the Trustees got jittery!

About five or six years after we started HHC the Trustees and several other people began asking when we were going to hand over the running of the charity and to whom. We knew that there must be a graveyard somewhere for the Founders of Charities who had been unceremoniously removed by their Trustees and we had no wish to join them. Succession planning became an issue and during the course of a Trustees' meeting some years later one of the 'senior' Trustees said, *"I can tell you, if we had to choose a new Chief Executive now, it would not be you."* Just in time, as Mark was about to storm out of the room, the said Trustee went on to explain that he thought we had a more important role to play in the future as Ambassadors.

Both of us are keen sailors and the analogy struck us that the charity was like a yacht under sail. The wind was blowing strongly in our favour; we were going faster and faster, but we didn't know where we were going or how we were going to get there. So, we decided we had to jump ship before hitting a rock and sinking.

We arranged a meeting with our Chairman at the time, Matt Bell, and told him of our decision. We rather expected him at least to pretend that he was sorry and attempt to make us change our minds. But he didn't! He smiled happily and said, *"Good. You're ahead of the game as usual."* At midnight on 31 December 2005 we handed over our precious 'yacht' to a new 'skipper', Rick Foulsham, and we went off to Australia for a month to enjoy our son Edward's wedding to Sonya.

From a huge list of applications we were delighted that Rick Foulsham had been appointed as the new CEO. He had recently retired from an extremely successful career in the Foreign and Commonwealth Office. He quickly took 'the helm' and settled 'the ship' by proceeding to put in place all those things which we had neglected. When we came back we were very definitely 'lower deck crew members'.

The Trustees decided that we should be given the rather pretentious titles of Founder Presidents and continue to work in the office in East Clyffe as Ambassadors, Advocates and Advisers, in support of Rick. We were very happy with this arrangement, even though several people warned us of possible difficulties ahead. They thought it was inevitable that we would very quickly have a major disagreement with the new CEO which would be terminal for him or for us. To minimise the risk of this happening, we took the decision to undertake only the work that he asked us to do and not to interfere in the decision-making process unless our opinion was sought.

Our intent was tested almost to breaking point when Rick and the Trustees decided to change our logo. The lovely smiling face of a house surrounded by a heart was to be replaced by a heart with blue scribble all over it. We were told the old one was far too whimsical, not modern enough. We were very upset by this, as were a large number of our most loyal supporters. It caused considerable resentment at the time. However, we decided that we had no option but to accept this decision as it did not alter our work with the children in any way.

Although on his appointment in January 2006 Rick made it clear that, for him, six years as CEO seemed about the right length of time, we were surprised and disappointed when he told us one day early in 2011 that he thought it was time for him to hand over to someone else. We disagreed and tried unsuccessfully to persuade him to stay on longer. As a small children's charity HHC was developing well and was growing in strength with highly competent staff in the UK and overseas. We are enormously grateful to him for his total commitment from day one and putting his heart and soul into all he did. We were sorry to see him go and despite the prophets of doom who warned us that we would 'fall out' soon after we handed over to him, we still remain the best of friends.

In October 2011 Mark Waddington took over from Rick as the new CEO. Mark was CEO of War Child before he joined us. He had spent all his working life in the voluntary sector and knows far more about NGOs than we ever will! Shortly after his appointment we had dinner with him one evening in a local pub. He took us by surprise when he told us that he realised when he had been running War Child that no-one could ever stop wars. Then he went on to say, *"But we (HHC) could close all the institutions for children in the world."* Our reaction was one of incredulity, similar to that when Caroline said ten years earlier that her dream was to close all the institutions in Romania. After a second bottle of red wine, it didn't seem such a big problem. In fact, the more we talked, it became clear that this was where all our work and experience was leading. We had never thought about such an ambitious goal before – and suddenly it became obvious. Mark (C) said it sounded like the Rotary International aim 'to eradicate polio'; eradication is such a powerful, unequivocal and motivating word. Together the three of us agreed that the eradication of institutional care of children should be our global goal. Thus, the future vision of HHC was decided, over dinner and two bottles of wine – or maybe it was three!

We were, of course, aware of the growing interest in DI. In 2007 Georgette Mulheir had co-authored the European Commission's publication on *De-institutionalising and Transforming Children's Services*, but we had never envisaged HHC playing such a key role as advocate and practitioner in this vitally important work.

Mark (W) spent much of the next year discussing ideas with staff and Trustees, and writing concept papers and business plans which led to Our Vision,'*A world in which children no longer suffer institutional care*'. At the end of January 2013 all our Country Directors came to Salisbury and we held a meeting on 29 January attended by them, our Trustees and UK staff. This new Vision, and Our Mission '*To be the catalyst for the global eradication*

Mark Waddington explaining another new strategy at a staff meeting

of institutionalised care of children', was announced to everyone along with our strategic plans of how we intended to achieve this. As Mark (C) said, "*This is an historic moment in the history of the charity. It marks the end of the beginning and the beginning of the end of HHC. When we have eradicated institutionalised care, there will be no more need for our work.*"

The only problem for both of us was that Mark (W) kept saying that we could do this within our lifetime. Considering our age, we told him that it may be a little too ambitious, but hopefully it might be possible within our grandchildren's lifetime. Thus the dedication at the beginning of the book reflects this, our new dream.

None of us is pretending for one minute that we can achieve this on our own. That is why our HHC Mission clearly states that we are going to be the catalyst for the global eradication of institutional care of children. Such an enormous goal can only be attained if decision-makers and activists work together.

Children are still the heart of HHC's work and remain the key focus, but we have moved on a long way from the start 20 years ago when we were dealing with just a few children who we knew personally. In the early days we often used to discuss together whether we really wanted the charity to grow bigger. We felt a close connection with the children we were helping – we knew them and we visited them regularly. If HHC grew, it was inevitable that we would become increasingly detached from the children and we wondered if this was what we really wanted. We did not. But we realised that if we could help more children, we were morally bound to do so. If we could save 1,000 children's lives, why limit ourselves to 100 just because it would be easier and allow us to have a personal involvement in their future?

HHC continues to develop and, as with any organisation, changes and improvements take place. We believe no other organisation in the world has our depth of practical experience in reforming a country's institutional-based care into family-based care for vulnerable children. We must continue to be practitioners as well as advocates. At the start we had no experience and no credibility, now we have both. We really are being the catalyst for change.

A large part of HHC's current work focuses on advocacy, on technical assistance, training and closing institutions. We are working at the highest level with Governments, the EU, UNICEF and many other organisations to raise awareness of the physical, cognitive and emotional damage to children and the ongoing cost and negative impact of institutionalisation. We work hard to persuade them to support the necessary changes. We are also giving advice and training to people who have to make those changes a reality. And, most importantly, we help vulnerable families by putting in place all the appropriate alternative services while closing State institutions. For us, personally, our hearts and our passion still remain with the children and their families.

❧

❧
Our HCC Family

Patrons

From the start we have been incredibly lucky that so many eminent people have agreed to be Patrons. One of the first was Lord Carrington who we met for lunch. We explained our intentions and ideas and he immediately said that he would do anything he could to support us. He has been true to his word and an amazingly generous and active Patron ever since. Our number of Patrons has grown over the years as other notable people with various skills, experience and contacts have joined us.

Our Patron, Lord Carrington, opening the West Wing, former lambing sheds

We did not realise the importance of Trustees until we filled in the form to become a Registered Charity. We wrote that we were going to run the charity and that, initially, we would appoint three Trustees. The written response from the Charity Commission was, *'You cannot appoint Trustees, but they may appoint you!'* Michael Nicholson agreed to become our first Chairman and Ken Groves and an old friend, Deirdre Green, agreed to be Trustees. None of us had any experience in setting up and running a charity. It was only when they told us that we could not go to Rwanda during the genocide that we realised that, once again, we were not masters of our own destiny.

Over the years we have been fortunate to have many dedicated Trustees who have willingly given an enormous amount of their time, experience and expertise to guide the charity's development. There are too many to mention by name, but in succession the Chairmen were Michael Nicholson, Ken Groves, Andrew Baines, Mike Milan, Matt Bell and currently Tim Richards. We may not have agreed with all their decisions, but admit, in hindsight, that they were usually right! The strong governance that they put in place has ensured the growth, development and future of HHC.

Ken Groves has also played a vital role in helping to organise every one of our twenty annual Carol Concerts in London, and, with his wife Violet, has also decorated the Church every year.

An early Trustees' meeting in the office with Andrew Baines, James Whiting, Matt Bell, Mike Milan, Deirdre Cain, Ken Groves, Michael Stewart and Felicity Craven

We had hoped that following Mark's announcement of starting HHC to the 5,000 women in the Royal Albert Hall we would be deluged with offers of support. We weren't! In fact we heard nothing for over two months. And then a man telephoned us to say that his wife had heard Mark speak at the event and invited us to give a presentation at a Rotary District Conference to an audience of about 1,000 people in Harrogate. Of course we accepted eagerly. We knew little of Rotary then, but we do now!

Our Patron, Martin Bell, speaking on behalf of HHC at one of many Rotary events

The District Governor, Jim Suthering, became a great supporter and ambassador for us. Following on from the Harrogate conference we were adopted by the RIBI President, Rodney Huggins in 1996 and Neil Hill in 1997 as their 'preferred international charity'. Many of us in HHC have talked at literally hundreds of Rotary and Inner Wheel events and Clubs around the country and abroad since then, including in Eritrea, Albania, Sudan and Romania. They are both incredible, global organisations. The Rotary's motto is 'Service before Self'. Over the last 19 years Rotary and Inner Wheel have raised more than £3 million for us. In addition, many have become great personal supporters. Without their enthusiastic support we would not be in the position we are in today.

Mark is proud to be an Honorary Member of Frome Selwood Rotary Club and a Paul Harris Fellow.

Our Patron, Gordon McInally, with children in Sudan

St. James's Place (SJP)

One afternoon whilst working in the office on our own, the telephone rang and Caroline answered it. After a very long conversation she told the caller that if she watched television that evening, she would see and hear more about our work as Mark had been ambushed by Michael Aspel on the programme *This Is Your Life* two days earlier and it was being screened that night. When she put the phone down Mark asked who it was and Caroline said, *"A lady called Gail Mitchell-Briggs from J. Rothschild Assurance."* We were very excited! The next day Gail called back and invited us for an interview with the Board. She explained that they had a Foundation which supported children's causes, but had never supported charities working with children overseas before as there was a feeling amongst some of their committee that the money would probably just disappear.

Gail Mitchell-Briggs

Mark Waddington, second left, with Ian Jamieson, Mike Wilson and Martin Rashdi from SJP

A few days later we met the Board and told the members that, if they supported us, we would willingly take any of them to see one of our projects. They decided to give us £125,000 to buy six homes in Ukraine. Mark took out a party of four committee members for the opening of the homes some months later. This was the start of our biggest corporate partnership which has subsequently grown in strength and

Martin, Mike and Mark (W) in a home in Ukraine

David Bellamy, SJP's CEO, with his two sons after completing the Triathlon

importance. Some time later they changed their name to Saint James's Place; their Foundation now raises over £3 million every year through regular donations from partners for many children's charities. They also organise and take part in numerous, often very challenging, fundraising events such as an annual triathlon, Iron Man competitions, swimming the English Channel, and various expeditions. SJP has been an inspiration to us and we now have many good friends in the organisation. Over the last 15 years they have raised nearly £6 million for us and numerous partners have been to visit the programmes in the different countries they have supported.

Gail Mitchell-Briggs went to Ukraine for the opening of the first home funded by SJP and was very excited that her telephone call to Caroline had resulted in such a strong partnership between our two organisations. Sadly Gail died in 2006. Her husband, Nick, went out to Ukraine with the SJP party for the opening of the Ray of Hope Centre in Makariv. Nick opened the home next to it which we named after Gail. It was very moving for all of us there who knew and loved Gail.

ABSOLUTE RETURN FOR KIDS (ARK)

The support that ARK has given us in Romania has been truly amazing. The impact of it has gone far wider than in that country alone. It has become the global model of how to reform a country's childcare system. This would never have happened without ARK's most generous support and commitment.

Individual Donors

Right from the start of HHC we have been overwhelmed by the kindness and generosity of supporters and donors who have made our work possible. They gave us enormous encouragement in the early days and made a huge difference to our confidence. In the beginning the majority of our donors were individuals and we responded personally to their gifts. One of our long-term supporters wrote to us recently and said, *'Our support dates back from a television programme. We thought that you were doing really important work and that you would make a great success of it. It is always nice to be proved right!'*

Our first HHC Christmas card in 1994, one of many painted by a great friend, Pippa Watt

Support Groups

As a result of the extensive coverage in the *EDP*, many people in East Anglia started supporting us. A retired Norfolk headmaster, Alan Childs, telephoned us one day and said he would like to start a Support Group. We had no idea what he meant, so we arranged to meet him in a pub. He outlined his idea of organising a group of supporters to hold events to promote our work and raise funds. Alan started the East Anglian Support Group and many others followed his lead and formed Support Groups around the country. The East Anglian Support Group is still amazingly supportive as are our many dedicated and active Support Groups throughout the UK. To date they have raised the staggering sum of over £3 million.

SCHOOLS

Soon after we started HHC we felt that it was important to tell children in schools about our work with some of the poorest children in the world, many of whom may never have the chance of an education. We have spoken to countless schools from prep and primary to universities across Europe: their enthusiastic response and their initiatives to help these children have been an inspiration to us. Unfortunately there are too many to name them all, but we would like to mention the following: Coopers' Company and Coburn School has supported us every year from our beginning in 1994 raising £85K; Wellington College raised nearly £150K in celebration of their 150th Anniversary; Doha English Speaking School has raised £124K, and schools in London owned by Michael Loveridge £163K. To date schools have raised the magnificent sum of over £2 million. They have been responsible for transforming the lives of many hundreds of children and given them the chance to go to school too. Several ex-students have continued to support us; one, Tom Dannatt, mentioned in the chapter on Sierra Leone, has even started his own children's charity.

VOLUNTEERS

Volunteers in this country and overseas have played a key role in many different ways including fundraising, helping in the office, creating Support Groups, organising events, giving talks and working in our programmes overseas. Over the years, they have saved us an enormous amount of money by taking on tasks which we would, otherwise, have had to pay for, and they have raised literally millions of pounds. In the early years we had an overseas programme in which volunteers helped in the orphanages we were closing. We also had a number of volunteers with specialist skills – these included physiotherapists, occupational therapists and aromatherapists. They frequently took unpaid leave or went out to the countries in their holiday time to work with the local staff and children and share their skills. They were very useful in helping the children who had been very badly physically and psychologically damaged.

OVERSEAS STAFF

We have been particularly lucky in recruiting many truly exceptional local people in the countries in which we have worked. The majority of them are highly intelligent, hardworking and totally dedicated to helping the most vulnerable children in their country, and they all have a deep desire to reform their childcare system. Inevitably they work in extremely difficult and sometimes hostile environments. Much of the success of HHC can be attributed to them; they are right on the 'frontline'. They make our work happen and our dreams come true.

A gathering of overseas and UK staff at our annual UK conference in 2001

UK Staff

One of the greatest challenges we have faced has been our staff in the UK office at East Clyffe. Mark's 31 years in the Gurkhas had not prepared him for this and we could write another book on the subject. Recruiting the right people and retaining them, while removing the wrong people, has taken up a great deal of time and caused considerable stress. The majority of our UK staff have been totally passionate and professional. But there have been some over the years whose aptitude and suitability bore little resemblance to their references from past employers. We learned in the early years that Caroline's 'gut feeling' about a person, her intuition, was a far better indication of whether they were suitable to become part of our small team, rather than being impressed by their references.

Since well over 250 people have worked in our East Clyffe office over the last 20 years, it would be impossible to mention all of them. However, there are a number of staff (not mentioned elsewhere in this book) who have been with us for ten years or more and whose contribution we would particularly like to acknowledge. These are:

Sue Rooke, our Director of Resources, has played a major role in the growth, development and accountability of the charity. Sue came to us with a great deal of experience having been Field Auditor for Save the Children. Knowing that Sue is there with her finger on the financial 'safety button' has given us, personally, great confidence and reassurance. We are greatly indebted to her. Kay Cooper, our Accounts Manager, was our first specialist finance person; she joined us in 1998. Sue Lees was appointed in 2000 as James Whiting's PA and for many years she has been Programmes Information Manager. Beth Maughan joined the Fundraising Team in 2004 and is currently Head of Marketing & Communications. Chris Daniels is Finance & International Travel Officer and Beth Hunt is Supporter Care Assistant. All of these members of staff have made a rich contribution to HHC over many years.

We realised at the start that the role of Receptionist was really important; for many people this person would be the first point of contact with the charity. We were very lucky that our dear friend Kay Dawson volunteered to be our HHC Receptionist. Her wonderfully warm, reassuring voice was a tremendous asset. Supporters frequently commented on how much they enjoyed talking to her. Kay made everyone feel they were very special. She played a vital role in our first ten years. She was, the 'Voice of HHC'.

Kay Dawson welcoming supporters to our East Clyffe office

Some of our staff, outside the main entrance to the office, advertising our 20th Birthday Party in 2014

HOPE BEAR

A very special member of our HHC Family is Hope Bear or just Bear for short. He was made by Kathleen Evershed who, with her husband Charles, was a regular volunteer in our East Clyffe office. We started taking him on our country visits. Not only did the children love him, but Bear was immediately popular with everyone who met him and was a great ice-breaker with the children and even Government officials. On one visit to Sierra Leone, Mark introduced him to the Paramount Chief of Makeni who was fascinated by him. On a subsequent visit, about a year later, the first question the Paramount Chief asked was, *"Where is Bear?"* One old man in Eritrea, who was herding goats, circled around Bear, carefully keeping his distance, and then asked if Bear was real. Mark had what he thought was another of his 'great fundraising ideas' and that was to write a series of books about Hope Bear's amazing adventures in all the countries he visited. Unfortunately we did not have the time to pursue this. Considering the popularity of teddy bears all around the world, we are still convinced that Hope Bear could become a global superstar! He is still 'alive' and having a break from his exhausting travels, but very keen to do whatever he can to help children.

A surprised Bear meeting a Harrods bear on an internal flight in Africa

Bear with a young friend in Eritrea

Very early on, many of our supporters donated money or organised their own fundraising events, either individually or in groups. It is, of course, not possible to mention every event as they were numerous and of a huge variety. Each and every one helped us to transform the lives of ever more children and develop our work further.

Our Patron Al Humphreys in the desert in Sudan

Some events over the past 20 years stand out because of their supreme physical effort and endurance. Alastair Humphreys spent over four years cycling around the world, a journey of 46,000 miles through 60 countries and across five continents. He visited several of our projects on the way and when he landed back in the UK on a Southampton ferry, he cycled up to our office in East Clyffe arriving in time for a cup of tea! It was raining, there was a headwind and his bike was falling to pieces. It was, he said, the worst leg of his whole journey! A few years ago he started organising *'Night of Adventure'* events with us. These very popular and successful events take place in different parts of the country.

Olly Hicks, had heard Mark speak at his school, Harrow, and decided to support us by rowing across the Atlantic from America to the UK. He was in his early twenties at the time and was aiming to become the 'youngest and fastest' person to complete the crossing from west to east. He was hit by terrible weather and was in great danger of becoming the 'oldest and slowest'. He ran out of food and was resupplied by a Royal Navy frigate which happened to be passing. But he did it and we eventually welcomed him back to Falmouth along with a large crew of supporters including Prince William and Richard Branson.

Olly in the Atlantic

Claire Wright has undertaken several extremely challenging runs including the *Marathon des Sables* (Sahara Marathon). Camilla Lee-Warner has also run several marathons for us; she and her husband Martin, an old school friend of Mark's, have been incredibly supportive from the start.

Martin Rashdi came up with the idea of organising an annual SJP triathlon

Our Patron Claire Wright in the Sahara

for us 12 years ago which has, so far, raised nearly £1.5 million. Many SJP partners have undertaken extreme events on our behalf including swimming the English Channel and the North Pole Marathon and one of the partners, Jeremy Clay, has done both of them.

Someone suggested we should organise a fundraising trek to Everest Base Camp. Mark was quite certain that this was the last thing he wanted to do, but Caroline was very tempted to go in order to help raise much-needed funds. However, she realised that she would probably be the oldest person on the trek and she was anxious about her ability to take on such a challenge and worried about letting others down. After lengthy consideration she decided to put her name down for it and began a strict training regime to get fit and prepare herself for the challenge. We spent days with our dog Asha, walking over the Wiltshire countryside. Sarah Bates (now Whiting and our Director of Fundraising) also decided to go; she and Caroline trained seriously together running up and down hills including along the South Coast and in Wales.

We had no idea how many people would be interested in such an endeavour. It needed at least 15 people to make it worthwhile and we were surprised and delighted by the response; 39 people took part and everyone made it to Base Camp which was an enormous achievement. At a celebratory dinner in Lukla on the last night, before they all flew back to Kathmandu from the tiny airstrip, Caroline was able to announce that between them they had raised the incredible sum of over £180,000.

Before they went on the trek Caroline and Sarah had decided that they would not make any contact with home – that no news was good news. On their return three weeks later Mark was shocked to see how much weight Caroline had lost. In her summary of the trip Caroline said that it had been an amazing three weeks, but one of the toughest things that she had ever had to do in her life. There were certain factors that had kept her spirits up during the trek – the stunningly beautiful scenery of snow-covered mountains and exhilarating glimpses of Everest; the comradeship of the other trekkers, particularly Sarah, her tent companion; and the amazing organisation of the trekking company leading them. But when things got tough her constant thought was remembering the heart-breaking sight of children she had seen imprisoned in State institutions. Every step taken was helping to raise the money needed to give more of these children love and freedom. All in all it was a hugely worthwhile trip and Caroline said she will never, ever, forget the richness of such an experience … but would never do it again!

Following the success of this, we organised another trek to Base Camp, one to the Inca Trail in Peru, two up Mount Kilimanjaro in Kenya, and a bike ride in Vietnam. All these raised huge sums of money and increased the profile of the charity by attracting participants who were new to us and had to get their own sponsors. Many of these people are still supporting us.

Caroline and Sarah celebrating their arrival at Base Camp

One of our supporters donated free advertising space on London buses and underground stations.

One of the posters placed in London underground stations
Photograph by Oggi

Larry Hollingworth, who worked with us for a short while, Mark,
Martin Bell and James in front of a special bus displaying our logo
and an advertisement designed by Sam Taylor-Johnson

Ambushed by Michael Aspel on 'This Is Your Life' - 1999

We have been lucky … incredibly lucky … that so many people have trusted and supported us over the last twenty years. We have written this book specifically to thank you all. Many of you have become very good friends along the way and we feel blessed by this priceless, and totally unforeseen, gift.

We hope you have enjoyed reading our book and you are pleased that you decided to support us. People sometimes say to us, *"You should be proud of all you have achieved."* Far from it, we really are not. We are far too conscious of the things we could have done better, the mistakes we have made, the people we have hurt and the children we have failed, to feel any sense of pride.

Also, we have not done this alone; it really has been a wonderful team effort. Our UK staff and overseas country teams have been truly amazing in their total commitment and their incredible hard work, often in very difficult situations. Always their love for the children has sustained them and spurred them on. And most importantly you, our supporters, have given us the resources to make it all possible.

The first ten years were very exciting – intoxicating even. Nothing seemed impossible. We saw a need in a country and went out to try and help. At no time did we wonder where the money would come from – we just knew that it would. Fundraising was the means to the end – the children were our motivating force. After every country visit we came back re-energised and increasingly passionate.

HHC is now a very professional organisation run with all the appropriate governance and procedures of a successful, sustainable charity. This had to happen for it to survive and we are happy about it. But for us now with only a peripheral role and without that personal contact with the children, our flame is flickering as, regrettably, is our energy! We have handed over the torch to others to keep it alive and burn even more brightly. Our race is over. We feel unbelievably privileged to have been given this opportunity in our lives to do something so positive. We are truly grateful for your love and support.

We thank you all most sincerely.

Mark & Carolina.

A Christmas card painted by 14 year old Alexander Sentsov

"The candle that they (the Cooks) have lit seems to offer precious little light in the darkness that threatens to envelope many of the world's children. But if others light similar candles it will grow less dark. There is no knowing what the love Hope and Homes for Children seeks to arouse in the human heart might achieve in a hard world."

Lord Bill Deedes in the *Daily Telegraph*

࿙

HOPE & HOMES FOR CHILDREN

		TOTAL 20 years £	Year ended 31-Dec-13 £	Year ended 31-Dec-12 £	Year ended 31-Dec-11 £	Year ended 31-Dec-10 £	Year ended 31-Dec-09 £	Year ended 31-Dec-08 £	Year ended 31-Dec-07 £
Income									
Fundraising income									
Individuals	23.04%	18,289,027	1,067,145	1,337,365	1,433,045	1,670,395	1,277,196	1,556,514	1,344,679
Corporates	12.99%	10,312,934	632,706	595,065	716,891	1,034,211	1,117,930	996,490	920,044
Charitable trusts and foundations	18.62%	14,782,278	2,474,481	1,226,081	2,066,298	1,439,196	1,245,486	1,145,964	972,933
Community groups	10.33%	8,202,352	132,589	244,775	455,725	610,655	522,847	443,128	240,560
Support group activities	4.48%	3,553,184	88,371	144,995	154,291	177,539	215,143	392,981	295,591
Event fundraising	4.26%	3,379,022	441,809	396,950	341,814	231,393	167,232	195,371	221,368
Trading	0.42%	332,169	9,911	7,820	9,498	10,197	10,719	13,073	18,622
sub-total		*58,850,966*	*4,847,012*	*3,953,051*	*5,177,562*	*5,173,586*	*4,556,553*	*4,743,521*	*4,013,797*
Other funding									
Legacies	3.68%	2,923,983	489,001	151,764	135,506	266,673	1,000,026	186,563	126,902
Absolute Return for Kids	13.81%	10,964,982	917,501	1,232,305	1,555,982	366,364	1,571,425	215,240	1,294,196
In-country funding	7.89%	6,261,344	1,577,436	844,459	1,244,535	564,909	340,636	196,365	310,217
Investment income	0.48%	379,358	2,502	4,362	4,048	8,311	6,211	21,321	54,809
Total	100%	79,380,633	7,833,452	6,185,941	8,117,633	6,379,843	7,474,851	5,363,010	5,799,921
Expenditure									
Fundraising	18.66% 19.66%	14,815,006	939,107	1,085,017	1,393,427	1,325,392	1,213,914	1,429,460	1,233,735
Overseas programmes									
Eritrea	0.90%	*680,252*	*0*	*0*	*0*	*0*	*19,225*	*42,344*	*85,757*
Mozambique	0.51%	*386,907*	*0*	*0*	*0*	*0*	*0*	*0*	*0*
Rwanda	7.23%	*5,448,502*	*821,742*	*682,639*	*579,854*	*696,365*	*487,252*	*492,508*	*519,720*
Sierra Leone	7.10%	*5,349,048*		*78,598*	*263,545*	*332,085*	*335,075*	*413,926*	*537,490*
South Africa	5.03%	*3,788,514*	*58,913*	*322,550*	*676,441*	*639,678*	*404,163*	*338,732*	*332,980*
Sudan	5.52%	*4,160,887*	*281,785*	*225,385*	*213,793*	*256,934*	*350,207*	*490,255*	*647,145*
Albania	1.84%	*1,383,995*	*9,071*	*7,953*	*6,332*	*7,446*	*10,113*	*8,472*	*29,991*
Belarus	1.92%	*1,448,647*	*68,644*	*58,543*	*69,833*	*114,036*	*78,970*	*102,445*	*185,299*
Bosnia	4.82%	*3,634,099*	*246,161*	*225,269*	*326,888*	*295,215*	*336,306*	*339,760*	*311,844*
Bulgaria	0.98%	*738,711*	*438,833*	*154,717*	*72,257*	*72,904*	*0*	*0*	*0*
Croatia	0.29%	*215,739*	*0*	*0*	*0*	*0*	*0*	*0*	*0*
Kosovo	2.24%	*1,688,212*	*0*	*0*	*0*	*0*	*0*	*12,118*	*351,345*
Moldova/Transdnistria	4.29%	*3,235,203*	*444,849*	*451,700*	*492,238*	*385,755*	*238,907*	*226,763*	*185,561*
Romania	30.39%	*22,905,282*	*3,648,374*	*3,568,196*	*2,745,402*	*2,374,384*	*1,938,113*	*1,462,552*	*1,610,688*
Ukraine	6.38%	*4,807,055*	*293,039*	*205,481*	*541,333*	*646,068*	*262,611*	*295,341*	*205,118*
Global initiatives	0.30%	*228,608*	*228,608*	*0*	*0*	*0*	*0*	*0*	*0*
sub-total 79.75%		*60,099,661*	*6,540,019*	*5,981,031*	*5,987,916*	*5,820,870*	*4,460,942*	*4,225,216*	*5,002,938*
Governance	0.59%	446,828	71,683	47,311	34,359	40,249	35,997	42,220	20,685
Total	100%	75,361,495	7,550,809	7,113,359	7,415,702	7,186,511	5,710,853	5,696,896	6,257,358
Net receipts/(payments)			282,643	-927,418	701,931	-806,668	1,763,998	-333,886	-457,437
BALANCE SHEET									
Fixed assets			2,536,470	2,823,469	2,997,713	2,828,728	3,262,652	2,425,895	2,415,681
Cash			1,331,425	909,159	1,342,099	1,093,897	1,509,522	615,887	944,199
Debtors/(Creditors)			140,518	-6,858	-12,748	28,632	-14,249	-47,855	-32,067
			4,008,413	3,725,770	4,327,064	3,951,257	4,757,925	2,993,927	3,327,813
Restricted funds			3,222,650	3,225,467	3,997,713	3,352,971	3,888,237	2,709,480	2,558,894
Designated funds			61,726	92,152	123,586	141,450	175,925	210,337	468,245
General funds			724,037	408,151	531,889	456,836	693,763	74,110	300,674
			4,008,413	3,725,770	4,653,188	3,951,257	4,757,925	2,993,927	3,327,813

Year ended 31-Dec-06 £	9 months 31-Dec-05 £	Year ended 31-Mar-05 £	Year ended 31-Mar-04 £	Year ended 31-Mar-03 £	Year ended 31-Mar-02 £	Year ended 31-Mar-01 £	Year ended 31-Mar-00 £	Year ended 31-Mar-99 £	Year ended 31-Mar-98 £	Year ended 31-Mar-97 £	Year ended 31-Mar-96 £	Year ended 31-Mar-95 £
1,338,567	1,134,845	1,519,767	753,744	668,028	799,733	557,340	607,605	406,993	404,106	194,308	147,960	69,692
1,175,129	602,448	830,183	562,874	287,156	134,775	155,455	450,672	36,353	25,254	16,252	17,896	5,150
532,165	735,776	481,278	448,958	418,419	561,095	353,669	193,146	269,237	76,413	73,931	60,676	7,076
419,169	586,004	567,804	444,342	901,259	549,036	475,292	538,069	636,870	241,857	105,989	57,866	28,516
323,111	294,764	416,407	269,685	326,147	291,219	89,933	50,267	18,960	3,532	248	0	
346,623	188,648	236,528	315,567	64,191	197,830	4,985	3,100	4,362	11,337	6,107	3,325	482
16,023	19,230	44,293	31,211	27,277	31,358	33,166	22,513	20,065			7,193	
4,150,787	*3,561,715*	*4,096,260*	*2,826,381*	*2,692,477*	*2,565,046*	*1,669,840*	*1,865,372*	*1,392,840*	*762,499*	*396,835*	*294,916*	*110,916*
90,984	98,800	174,541	25,432	77,908	85,900	0	5,385	0	8,598	0	0	0
1,100,000	125,000	717,861	1,085,595	783,513	0	0	0	0	0	0	0	0
347,656	168,120	218,680	201,035	247,296	0	0	0	0	0	0	0	0
39,353	39,093	26,801	14,366	21,805	14,278	44,374	32,035	25,424	12,536	4,044	3,019	666
5,728,780	3,992,728	5,234,143	4,152,809	3,822,999	2,665,224	1,714,214	1,902,792	1,418,264	783,633	400,879	297,935	111,582
1,154,387	821,156	1,168,038	**886,422**	**585,810**	**516,010**	**371,552**	210,790	153,545	132,220	108,104	67,901	19,019
85,376	*91,478*	*54,599*	*115,013*	*73,720*	*42,949*	*47,773*	*11,356*	*0*	*7,438*	*3,224*	*0*	*0*
0	*0*	*0*	*0*	*0*	*221*	*3,453*	*136,273*	*68,435*	*168,320*	*10,205*	*0*	*0*
317,141	*254,375*	*227,197*	*178,511*	*136,046*	*48,647*	*6,505*	*0*	*0*	*0*	*0*	*0*	*0*
462,309	*381,534*	*389,331*	*364,045*	*379,361*	*384,156*	*355,010*	*261,189*	*171,089*	*54,635*	*162,639*	*23,031*	*0*
393,750	*286,025*	*164,739*	*66,052*	*43,439*	*36,579*	*24,473*	*0*	*0*	*0*	*0*	*0*	*0*
579,770	*268,020*	*223,447*	*150,850*	*177,167*	*145,938*	*138,880*	*11,356*	*0*	*0*	*0*	*0*	*0*
57,575	*270,837*	*97,349*	*91,847*	*68,723*	*92,904*	*186,986*	*56,780*	*117,623*	*245,648*	*18,344*	*0*	*0*
91,178	*45,344*	*107,127*	*167,558*	*140,260*	*115,584*	*92,470*	*11,356*	*0*	*0*	*0*	*0*	*0*
196,183	*155,647*	*168,735*	*110,617*	*105,845*	*74,287*	*99,469*	*147,629*	*256,633*	*12,514*	*49,715*	*174,682*	*700*
0	*0*	*0*	*0*	*0*	*0*	*0*	*0*	*0*	*0*	*0*	*0*	*0*
0	*0*	*0*	*4,669*	*6,914*	*9,198*	*17,009*	*56,780*	*117,623*	*1,659*	*1,886*	*0*	*0*
277,916	*220,703*	*270,245*	*151,148*	*250,405*	*154,332*	*0*	*0*	*0*	*0*	*0*	*0*	*0*
142,960	*96,955*	*179,110*	*196,122*	*115,462*	*62,527*	*16,294*	*0*	*0*	*0*	*0*	*0*	*0*
1,168,808	*718,904*	*759,817*	*902,689*	*922,857*	*453,901*	*430,740*	*68,136*	*128,317*	*3,404*	*0*	*0*	*0*
246,773	*365,377*	*203,248*	*306,908*	*294,840*	*242,863*	*346,310*	*252,105*	*96,237*	*3,403*	*0*	*0*	*0*
0	*0*	*0*	*0*	*0*	*0*	*0*	*0*	*0*	*0*	*0*	*0*	*0*
4,019,694	*3,155,199*	*2,844,944*	*2,806,029*	*2,715,039*	*1,864,086*	*1,765,372*	*1,012,961*	*955,958*	*497,021*	*246,013*	*197,713*	*700*
20,134	24,720	30,650	19,115	17,087	12,321	11,062	6,335	5,744	1,271	3,589	2,296	0
5,194,215	4,001,075	4,043,632	3,711,566	3,317,936	2,392,417	2,147,986	1,230,086	1,115,247	630,512	357,706	267,910	19,719
534,565	-8,347	1,190,511	441,243	505,063	272,807	-433,772	672,706	303,017	153,121	43,173	30,025	91,863
2,110,352	1,533,427	1,522,171	919,183	723,697	210,439	112,754	41,392	12,212	0			
1,655,485	1,729,829	1,820,392	1,185,216	870,306	918,300	790,862	1,138,173	599,255	313,615	160,162	116,614	88,532
19,413	-12,572	-83,532	-35,879	33,274	-6,525	-54,209	103,614	-994	-6,159	-5,827	-5,452	-7,395
3,785,250	3,250,684	3,259,031	2,068,520	1,627,277	1,122,214	849,407	1,283,179	610,473	307,456	154,335	111,162	81,137
2,542,642	2,493,519	2,130,664	1,172,884	667,713	149,533	73,831	8,987	46,333	8,549	8,549		
642,551	381,268	393,475	714,108	310,246	205,392	30,000	30,000	200,000	30,000	30,000		
600,057	375,897	734,892	181,528	649,318	767,289	745,576	1,244,192	364,140	268,907	115,786	111,162	81,137
3,785,250	3,250,684	3,259,031	2,068,520	1,627,277	1,122,214	849,407	1,283,179	610,473	307,456	154,335	111,162	81,137

Who needs a calculator when you have pegs?

1. This is a simplification of these figures which have been slightly rounded up or down:

Raised	£80,000,000
Spent on Programmes	£60,000,000
Spent on Fundraising	£15,000,000
Spent on Governance	£500,000

2. It has always been our goal right from the start that 80% of all our expenditure should go directly on Programmes. As you will see, we missed this target by 0.25%!

3. To spend £15,000,000 on Fundraising may seem to be an excessive amount (it certainly does to us), but when one considers that this created £80,000,000, we think this was a good investment.

❧

We have always been very cautious about saying how many children we have helped. In fact, we have often been 'accused' of underestimating the total, long-term impact of our work. For the first ten years we spent little time on the monitoring and evaluation of our programmes. Since then, it has become a high priority and an analytical system has been put in place in all countries to record the information as accurately as possible.

In the course of a lifetime a person comes into contact with countless people. The impact that they make can be positive or negative. For the lucky people in life most contacts will be positive. But for those less fortunate, such as children who are deprived and unloved, the high probability is that they will be forced into crime and prostitution in order to survive. Their lives may be blighted by darkness, hatred and jealousy. The impact on them and on all those they meet will be totally negative. The cost to society, to local communities and the global world in which we all live, will be enormous. By changing just one of those lives, many other people will benefit. It is impossible to assess the total positive impact on humanity that giving a child a loving family has rather than life in a bleak institution.

As Halya, our Country Director in Ukraine, wrote recently, *'I am excited that we are helping to stop the suffering of the most vulnerable children and families in the world. The services that we create and promote are not only supporting those families and children, but also improving the lives of whole communities and beyond.'*

The figures opposite are our best estimate of the numbers of children with whom we have worked and had a direct impact on their lives.

In addition, we estimate that there are about one million children whose lives have been 'touched' indirectly through our advocacy, training and technical support programmes.

EUROPE	2004-2013 DIRECT BENEFICIARIES
ALBANIA*	52
BELARUS	1,326
BOSNIA	2,351
BULGARIA	1,138
CROATIA*	53
KOSOVO*	120
MOLDOVA	2,000
ROMANIA	10,480
TRANSNISTRIA	502
UKRAINE	2,529
AFRICA	
ERITREA	66
MOZAMBIQUE	120
RWANDA	6,803
SIERRA LEONE	3,526
SOUTH AFRICA	4,460
SUDAN	5,354
TOTAL	40,880

*FULL DATA UNAVAILABLE

"The Work of Hope and Homes for Children saves the lives of children. They are unique because they are the only organisation to be working on direct closures of institutions while building the capacities of national authorities to make the transition to family-based care, and to be working internationally to ensure that standards and best practice are rolled out. They achieve incredible impact by creating partnerships through which they are able to leverage large sums of money to cover the costs of transition from institutional care to family-based care.

"After almost twenty years of experience in developing their successful model Hope and Homes for Children is having a truly global impact that will benefit millions of children's lives."

Maria Herczog

Eurochild President and Rapporteur for the UN Committee on the Rights of the Child

❧

Hope & Homes for Children

If you would like to know more about the work of
Hope & Homes for Children
please visit www.hopeandhomes.org
If you are not already a member of our 'extended family'
we do hope you will be inspired to join us.

Hope & Homes for Children
East Clyffe
Salisbury
Wiltshire SP3 4LZ
United Kingdom

Tel: +44 (0) 1722 790111

Registered Charity No. 1089490

‌·

"Be ever watchful for the opportunity to shelter little children with the umbrella of your charity. For, as they must bear the burdens of our mistakes, so are they in their innocence the repositories of our hopes for the upward progress of humanity."

Extract from the last Will and Testament of Conrad N. Hilton